ENGINEERING
PROJECTS FOR YOUNG SCIENTISTS

PETER H. GOODWIN

ENGINEERING PROJECTS FOR YOUNG SCIENTISTS

A GROLIER COMPANY

PROJECTS FOR YOUNG SCIENTISTS
FRANKLIN WATTS I 1987
NEW YORK I LONDON I TORONTO I SYDNEY

Photographs courtesy of: UPI/Bettmann Newsphotos: pp.
12, 29 (bottom); Huffy Corporation: p. 17; Boeing: p. 18;
General Motors Corporation: pp. 19, 38; Frank Sloan: p.
21; Peter H. Goodwin: pp. 27, 29 (top), 33, 41, 65, 69,
73, 76, 78, 90, 99, 110, 111, 114; U.S. Army Photograph:
p. 31; Estes: p. 37; AP/Wide World Photos: pp. 42, 44;
Official U.S. Air Force Photo: p. 46; Carnegie Hall Corporation: p. 83; W. R. Grace & Co.: p. 87.

Library of Congress Cataloging-in-Publication Data

Goodwin, Peter, 1951-
Engineering projects for young scientists.

(Projects for young scientists)
Bibliography: p.
Includes index.

Summary: Presents practical problems and science
fair projects related to engineering and physics.
covering such subjects as force, friction, motion,
sound waves, light waves, and mechanics. I. Title
II. Series.
TA149.G66   1987   620'.0076   86-32528
ISBN 0-531-15130-1 (paper ed.)
ISBN 0-531-10339-0 (lib. bdg.)

CONTENTS

TO MY WIFE, SUSAN, WITH MANY
THANKS TO MY BROTHER, TONY

ENGINEERING
PROJECTS FOR YOUNG SCIENTISTS

1

PHYSICS
AND ENGINEERING

If you look around you, you can see applications of physics and engineering everywhere. Physics explains why things are the way they are, while engineering applies the physics to problems that need solutions. Most people use a car without thinking much about why it was built in a particular way. However, before it was built, the laws of physics had to be applied to its design. Before an idea becomes reality, someone has to "engineer" it.

Engineers work at selecting the best solution to a problem. They must work with scientific laws, but sometimes engineers find that things work even though they do not know exactly why. Engineers build automobile engines even though they don't know exactly how the gas burns inside the engine. Their knowledge goes only so far. For this reason, engineering requires experimentation as well as a knowledge of science.

Everyone has been an engineer while growing up. As a child, you probably built piles of blocks, applying the "science" you knew. You found that some methods enabled you to build taller piles, while others didn't. As you experimented, you learned some basic physics. You might not have been able to put into words exactly what you learned, but still you learned.

The word *physics* scares a lot of people, although physics is just the study of matter and energy. We all deal with matter—things—and we also have an idea of what energy is. The difficulty comes as more precise words—or equations—are used to describe the world. Physics requires mathematics, but you can understand a lot of

physics knowing only a little mathematics. Only a few of the investigations in this book require knowledge of more than basic math.

This book outlines the proper method for finding answers to questions you ask, gives you a chance to "do" physics, and suggests engineering problems you may want to solve. In trying the projects, you will learn to ask the right questions, design experiments, build various types of apparatus, and draw conclusions from the results. Chapters are divided into related topics. In each section you will find a little background material on the topic, some preliminary investigations, and ideas for projects. Each chapter concludes with additional projects.

All the investigations and projects are meant to be starting points, not closed, dead-end tasks. Some of the projects are suitable for a classroom science project. Others may work better as after-school or weekend projects. Many projects are appropriate for science fairs, provided you go about your experimentation in a scientifically acceptable fashion. Of course, you can do a project for any purpose you wish, provided you have the time, inclination, and ability. Some of the simple experiments can be expanded into complex projects. For example, if you like the idea of building a wind tunnel and investigating air friction, you could build a more sophisticated wind tunnel than the one proposed in the text and design and test rocket-ship models rather than automobile models.

All the experiments and projects deal with mechanics and waves. As much as possible, they involve things that can be seen in the world around us, for example, bridges, automobiles, musical instruments, and various kinds of lenses. In doing these projects, you may sometimes find that your idea does not give the hoped-for result. However, negative results can be as meaningful as

UNDER CONSTRUCTION IN 1962—
THE PAN AM BUILDING IN NEW YORK CITY.

positive ones. The failures are necessary to point you in the right direction. Sometimes, too, you will find a good solution that leads to further questions. You may even discover something that no other engineer or scientist has ever discovered.

Many students are involved in various kinds of science contests other than science fairs. Two of these are physics olympics events and the Science Olympiad. These contests test your abilities to solve various sorts of problems. Information on such contests is given in Chapter 6.

Now that you have some idea of what you're in for, it's time to find something that interests you and start working. Oh, one more thing: don't forget to have fun!

2

WORKING
SCIENTIFICALLY

Scientists and engineers try to solve problems that interest them. They ask questions and seek the answers through experimentation.

Generally, scientists and engineers follow the scientific method of investigation. They form a *hypothesis* that guides them in their investigation. A hypothesis is a tentative answer to the problem which needs to be tested by experiment. If it is impossible to test the hypothesis, the hypothesis is essentially meaningless. You must be able to devise experiments to prove or disprove your hypothesis.

A child building a pile of blocks tests a hypothesis by placing a particular block in a particular place. The hypothesis is that the block will not cause the rest of the blocks to fall over. If the pile does not fall over, then the hypothesis is true and the child has gathered data to support the hypothesis. If the pile falls over, the hypothesis is false. The child notes the success or failure of the experiment and forms a new hypothesis: "I think another block goes on top of the last block."

As you work on *your* project, you will be forming and testing hypotheses. The data that you collect will either support these hypotheses or lead you to reject them. The questions you ask may have been asked before in slightly different ways, but your research is designed to answer your own questions.

You should run a *systematic* experiment in order to be able to interpret the results. For instance, if you wanted to test the hypothesis that you go faster down a hill on a bicycle if you crouch over the handlebars, you would need to ride down a hill sitting upright and then ride the bicycle down the same hill crouched over the handlebars. You would then compare the time that it took to go down the hill in each case. You change *only* one thing, one *variable*, keeping all other conditions as identical as possible: one time you are sitting upright, and one time you are crouching.

The question "Which method is faster?" is actually a poor question. It is not specific enough. Are you taking into account the wind or any other variables? A wind blowing from behind you would actually make you go faster if you were sitting upright on the bicycle. Therefore, the answer depends on the question that you ask. Be precise in formulating your question. Good scientists ask precise questions. Designing your experiment carefully will increase your chances of getting useful results.

OBTAINING AND USING DATA

After you have decided what you want to investigate and have developed a hypothesis, you must design an experiment to test it. The experiment must be able to yield a sufficient quantity of data of sufficient accuracy to enable you to either accept or reject your hypothesis. This may require you to build an apparatus that will allow you to obtain data of the desired accuracy.

For example, some experiments require you to measure time to the nearest minute. Others might require you to measure it to the nearest hundredth of a second. How precisely do you need to measure the time required to go down the hill on the bicycle? Can you get good enough data with a watch that measures to the nearest second, or do you need one that measures more precisely?

After you get your data, you must determine the significance of your results. This can become quite mathematical, and for some experiments you may need the assistance of someone familiar with statistics in order to see if your numbers have any real meaning. However, for

AN EXPERIMENTAL BICYCLE. WHAT ADVANTAGE
MIGHT THERE BE IN THE ABSENCE OF SPOKES?

most projects, it is possible to see differences easily if the data are reasonably precise.

If you analyze your data and find that you cannot really conclude anything from them, you may have to redesign your experiment to get better data. Again using the experiment with the bicycle, could the wind be causing problems? Is anything else causing the confusing results? After you have run the experiment once, you will have a better idea of the kind of data you need. You also will know the kind of data you get from the apparatus that you used. This should help you the next time you run the experiment.

Once you have reached a conclusion about your hypothesis, you might end your research. However, you might also find that your results raise more questions than they answered. Would a different bicycle give the same results? Does the steepness of the hill matter? How does the weight of the person affect the result?

FULL-SIZE MOCK-UP OF THE U.S. SUPERSONIC TRANSPORT,
WHICH NEVER DID GO INTO PRODUCTION.

As you can see, results from one experiment may lead to other experiments. This is true of scientific research in general. At some point, however, you must make your project presentable to an audience even though you may continue with your research. This is true for professional scientists as it is for students. For a student, the presentation may involve showing the apparatus, graphs, pictures, and written results, perhaps at a science fair.

Scale models may be useful in your investigations. Engineers work with materials and try to design better structures and models to simulate the real world. Models are less expensive than "full-scale" machines, so you can test more designs for your money.

Using models presents some problems for the model builder. A full-scale version of the model may not behave quite like the model. If you build a one-tenth scale model (one unit of length for every ten units in the full scale), you may find that the forces, velocities, or other variables are not one-tenth their actual quantity. For this reason, you must be careful in drawing conclusions.

3

FORCES
AND MOTION

Mechanics is basic to the study of physics and engineering. Mechanics describes the forces exerted on all structures, how things move, and how forces affect motion. Building a house or a car involves a thorough knowledge of mechanics.

When engineers design a car, they must build it so that it won't fall apart under the stress of driving. They must also make sure that it handles properly and is comfortable for the passengers. In order for the car to hold

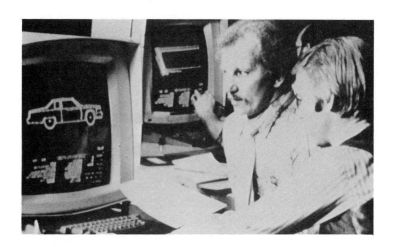

COMPUTERS PLAY A MAJOR ROLE TODAY
IN AUTOMOBILE DESIGN.

together, engineers must understand the forces exerted on it when it is driven. To make it handle and able to start and stop properly, they must know how these forces affect the motion of the car. And to make the car comfortable, the engineers must be aware of how a human body functions. For example, designing a comfortable seat requires a knowledge of human anatomy.

Engineers also work toward designing more efficient cars. For example, they try to reduce air friction because it reduces gasoline consumption. Engineers have found that using "molded" or "streamlined" mirrors saves gas; the old-fashioned mirrors stuck out from the car and disturbed the smooth flow of air past the car body. As a result, most new cars have the molded mirrors.

The following projects in the area of mechanics are only a few of the projects possible. They can be expanded by questions that arise from the results of the experiments. "If such and such happens when I do *this*, then what will happen if I change *that*?" Think about how your project could more completely investigate the motion or forces involved.

BRIDGES

Bridges have been built for thousands of years. A small bridge might be a log or board placed across a small stream, while the George Washington Bridge or the Golden Gate Bridge is quite a bit bigger and far more complex. All bridges have the same function, however: to allow travel over some obstacle. The design and construction methods vary dramatically depending on what is to travel across the bridge, what materials are available, and how long the bridge is.

Investigating the behavior of boards used for simple bridges is quite easy. Using scale models, you can build bridges with different designs and see which are the strongest and cheapest. As you build your models, think about bridges that you have seen. Develop a hypothesis to try to predict how to build the strongest bridge with the least expense. Then see if your hypothesis for an effi-

A SUSPENSION BRIDGE.

cient design actually works by running an experiment to test it. Keep a notebook as you work and write a project report when you finish.

Start with simple designs and models. Then, work with more complex forms and other materials. Here are two beginning projects. In the first, you will explore the relationship between strength and how wood for a bridge is positioned.

Materials and Tools

8 C-clamps
8 small blocks of wood, 5 cm (2 inches) on a side
50 pieces of wood, 0.5 cm × 5 cm × 60 cm (¼ inch × 2 inches × 2 feet) (can be purchased as ''lathe'' in lumberyards)
2 tables
light rope, 1 m (3 feet) long
2 20-liter (5-gallon) buckets
sand, enough to fill 1 bucket
bathroom scale
saw
drill and drill bits

Assuming that you have a large supply of wood, start with a simple "bridge." Use the C-clamp and blocks of wood to secure one piece of knotless wood between two tables. Make sure the wood can't move. Use the rope to secure the empty bucket to the center of the bridge. See Figure 1.

Add sand to the empty bucket until the wood bends downward 1 cm (½ inch). Use the scale to find the weight of the bucket and sand. Record this amount and then add sand until the wood breaks.

Start your experiments with the supports separated by about 0.5 m (1½ feet). Then, vary the distance between the supports (longer and shorter) and find the weight to bend the wood 1 cm and then to break it. Record the results. Make sure that all these pieces of wood are free of knots. Otherwise, you do not have a

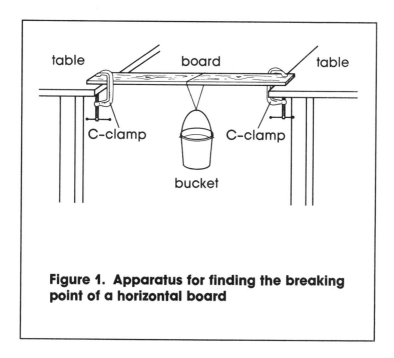

Figure 1. Apparatus for finding the breaking point of a horizontal board

controlled experiment. Then, repeat the experiment with the wood set up as shown in Figure 2.

Next, use the saw to cut a piece of wood lengthwise so the board is half as wide (2.5 cm, or 1 inch). Find the weight needed to bend it 1 cm and then the weight needed to break it. Is the change what you would predict it to be? How much change is there in the force when the dimension is halved?

As you record your data, be as precise as possible. Include the distance between the supports, the size and position of the applied force, the dimensions of the wood, the weight to cause 1-cm bending, and the force required for breaking.

If you do not have a large enough supply of wood, you can get good data by just causing the bridge to bend 1 cm. You do not have to add enough weight to break the wood. Houses are designed by using a rule of

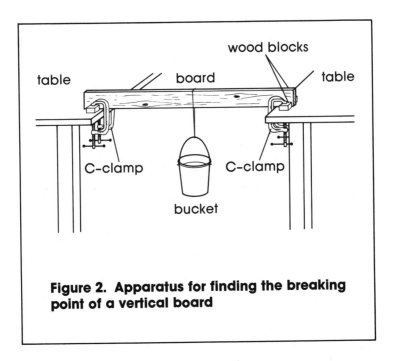

Figure 2. Apparatus for finding the breaking point of a vertical board

thumb that says you do not want to have the floor bend (move down) more than 1/360th of its length with a normal load on it. Otherwise the floor will feel too "springy" and is bothersome. Bridges are built so they bend less than about half the amount that a floor in a house bends.

In the second series of experiments, you will be investigating the effect of knots on the strength of your bridge. You will need the same materials as for the first experiment, plus the drill and drill bits.

Most wood has knots (places where limbs of the tree were), and these are weak points. When downward force is exerted on a board, the top part is in compression and the bottom is in tension (see Figure 3). The knot is strong when compressed but weak when under tension or when stretched. Under these circumstances, knots behave almost like holes in wood.

Using the same setup as before, investigate the effect of knots by drilling holes in the wood. Using real knots causes problems because all knots are not the same, and there is no control for your experiment. More precise data require more "uniform" knots. Drill the holes carefully so that the wood does not split.

Develop a hypothesis about where holes will weaken the bridge the most or the least. Then drill holes at various places, at the top, middle, and bottom, and at different distances from the supports. See if your ideas about the effect of knots was correct. If it was not, develop another hypothesis and experiment more.

After you have found how the position of a knot affects the strength of a bridge, vary the size of the holes but make them at least 0.5 cm (¼ inch) in diameter. Test these "knotty" bridges and find their breaking points. You may want to look at real bridges as you develop your hypotheses about how knots affect the strength of a bridge.

After you have experimented with the "uniform" knots made with a drill, find knots of the same size as the drilled holes and see if "real" knots behave in the same way as the drilled holes. Test a number of knots because no two knots will behave exactly the same.

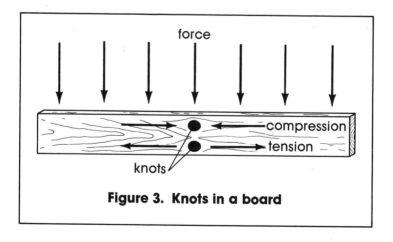

Figure 3. Knots in a board

PROJECTS WITH BRIDGES

1. A cantilever, as shown in Figure 4, is often used in construction, especially in the building of porches. Based on the experiments described above, design a porch using a cantilever which is safe and gives the largest floor area with the fewest construction materials. Develop a hypothesis for how far the board can be cantilevered and still be strong enough. Test your hypothesis by experiment.

2. Investigate the effect of a "truss" system on the strength of a bridge. Sample trusses are shown in Figure 5, but many more are possible. After you have done a little experimenting, hypothesize which truss systems are the strongest and then test your hypothesis. In building trusses, make sure the connections between pieces of wood are

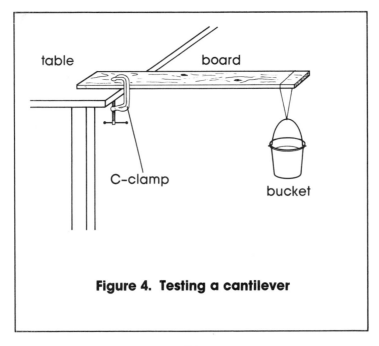

Figure 4. Testing a cantilever

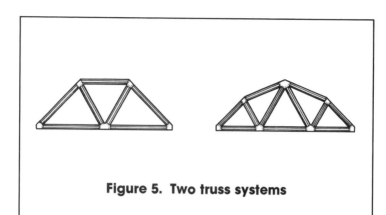

Figure 5. Two truss systems

A TRUSS BRIDGE.

strong so that they do not break before the wood does. Glue the pieces of wood together. Small nails or staples will help hold the wood together until the glue dries.

3. Investigate arches or domes for strength. The Romans used arches extensively, and eggs are strong because of their dome shape. Develop and test arches of your own design to see how strong they are.

4. Design the strongest bridge that you can with a fixed amount of wood.

5. Build a suspension bridge to find out why this kind of bridge can span large distances with the minimum of materials. Is a suspension bridge the strongest, most cost-effective such structure? Can you design an experiment to prove or disprove your answer?

6. Investigate how horizontal forces affect your bridge. A common horizontal force on a bridge is the wind. Examine how a variable wind affects the bridge. After you have run a few experiments, design a bridge that will be affected less by a strong wind. Build a model to test your ideas.

7. With the knowledge you have obtained from building other bridges, build the strongest bridge that you can to span 2 m (6 feet) using balsa wood and string.

8. Try to model your bridges on a computer and allow the computer to design bridges for you or help in making your models. This should be attempted only if you are very familiar with the computer as well as with physics and mathematics.

9. The same principles are used in building houses as in building bridges. The floors and roof are supported between the walls or the foundation. They "span" the distance between their supports. The boards holding up the floor are called floor joists. They must be strong enough so they do not break when people walk around, or dance, or jump up

TOP: PART OF THE AUTHOR'S HOUSE
UNDER CONSTRUCTION. *BOTTOM:* CONSTRUCTION
WORK ON THE PAN AM BUILDING.

and down. But how is a floor built? What size boards are needed in a particular situation? How do boards behave under forces? Construct a floor and observe how the spacing and board size affect the strength. For this project, use cardboard for the floor surface and rest it on the floor joists. Then see how much sand the floor can support.

Note: Your project write-up should include mention of both your successes and failures. Indicate what makes a weak bridge and what makes a strong one. Pictures or drawings and the construction details are important in presenting your report.

Books on building houses such as Cole and Wing's *From the Ground Up* and Ching's *Building Construction Illustrated* (see Bibliography) are good sources of information on how a material's size affects its strength. These books may also help you to find better ways to support whatever needs to be supported.

MODEL ROCKETS: ACTION AND REACTION

Experiments using model rockets can be used to explore how real rockets behave. A rocket moves because mass forced out of the rear exerts a force on the rocket. More force is exerted when more mass is expelled per unit time and when the mass is expelled at a higher velocity.

If you are familiar with model rockets that burn fuel, you may want to run some experiments with them. **HOWEVER, UNDER NO CIRCUMSTANCES SHOULD YOU CHANGE**

THE CORPORAL, AN OLD (1954) SURFACE-TO-SURFACE GUIDED MISSILE. WHY DO YOU SUPPOSE THE FINS ARE SO SMALL?

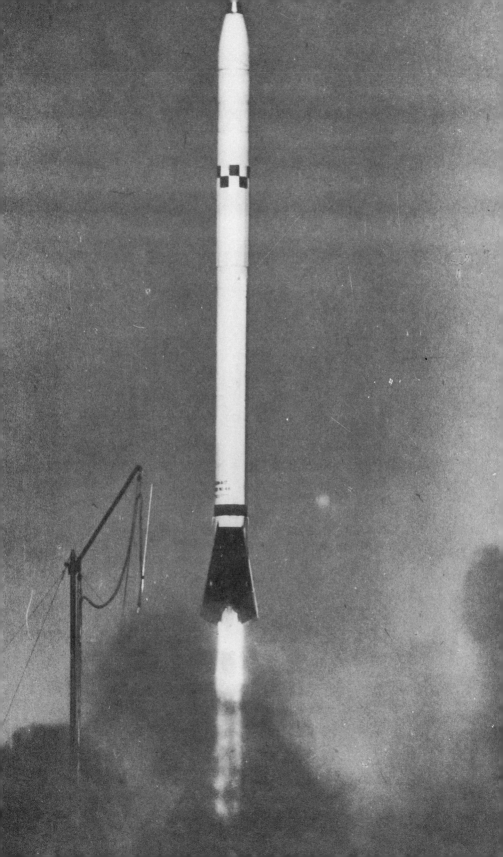

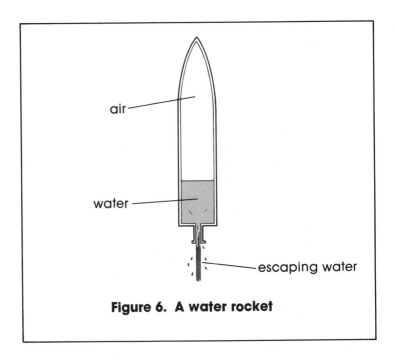

air

water

escaping water

Figure 6. A water rocket

THE AMOUNT OF FUEL OR MAKE MODIFICATIONS OTHER
THAN THOSE SPECIFIED BY THE MAKER OF THE ROCKET.
YOU MAY INJURE YOURSELF OR OTHERS. FOLLOW THE
MANUFACTURER'S INSTRUCTIONS AND OBEY ALL WARN-
INGS. IT MAY BE POSSIBLE TO USE DIFFERENT ENGINES FOR
YOUR EXPERIMENTS, BUT DO NOT MODIFY THEM. IF YOU
DECIDE TO USE FUEL-BURNING ROCKETS, WORK WITH THEM
UNDER THE SUPERVISION OF A QUALIFIED ADULT, FOR
EXAMPLE, YOUR SCIENCE TEACHER.

To avoid the danger of fuel-burning rockets, you are
encouraged to experiment with a "water rocket"
instead. Water is put in the rocket, and then air is
pumped into it. When the rocket is launched, the air
forces the water out and causes the rocket to rise (see
Figure 6). Water rockets are easy to use, and experiments with them can be repeated quickly. Also, they do

not fly as far as fuel-burning rockets, so measurements are easier because the rocket travels a small distance. You can buy a water rocket at a toy store.

HOW MASS AND PRESSURE AFFECT ROCKET FLIGHT

Get familiar with the rocket's operation and then start to gather data. You will be investigating the relationship between the amount of water and air pressure in the rocket's engine and the flight time and distance. You will be measuring the following: mass of the rocket, mass of the water added, the height to which the rocket rises, and the air pressure in the rocket. Use pressures and fuel quantities that make the rocket go only to heights that you can measure easily.

THE WATER ROCKET USED IN SOME
OF THIS CHAPTER'S EXPERIMENTS.

If your rocket rises about 5 m (15 feet) when fired vertically, collecting data will be relatively easy. You can measure the altitude attained by hanging a string out of a window with large markers on it every half meter or every foot. When the rocket is fired, the altitude attained can be compared with the length of string.

Air pressure can be measured quite precisely by the following method. Find the maximum length of the pump stroke by pulling the pump handle out as far as possible and then find how far the pump moves in. The distance the pump lever moves is related to the volume in the pump. Pushing the pump in halfway reduces the volume to half its original value. Pushing the pump three-quarters of the way in reduces the volume to one-quarter, etc. Halving the volume doubles the pressure. With one-quarter the volume, the pressure is quadrupled.

The pump is designed so that if the pressure in the pump is larger than the pressure in the rocket, air moves into the rocket. Therefore, you can measure the pressure in the rocket by finding the pressure when air starts bubbling into the rocket. You can use the relationship between volume and pressure to make a pressure scale on your pump as shown in Figure 7. Generally a small amount of water is used in the rockets, so the air pressure

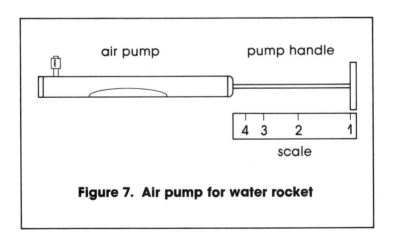

Figure 7. Air pump for water rocket

does not change much as the water is forced out. For the purposes of these experiments, the small change in pressure can be ignored.

You can now start to experiment. Add a small amount of water to the rocket, recording the amount of water. Pump the rocket to a predetermined pressure and measure how high the rocket flies straight up. Do this a number of times to get an average value for the height. Putting precisely the same amount of water in each time may be tricky but needs to be done in order to get good data.

Then, change the amount of water and observe the results. Try launching the rocket first with a small amount of water and then with a large amount. Plot your results on a graph: amount of water against height flown.

Next, double the pressure and observe the changes that occur with the new pressure.

PROJECTS WITH ROCKETS

1. Predict and then determine the relationship, if any, between the mass of the rocket and the maximum height. It may be possible to do this by taping extra mass onto the rocket. Some rockets have extra "stages"; these can be used for extra mass.

2. Obtain two different kinds of rockets with different-size openings where the water moves out. What differences, if any, occur when water leaves the rocket at a given pressure but through larger or smaller openings? Develop a hypothesis and then run experiments to test it. Compare rockets of the same mass and with the same pressure so that you change only one variable.

    It may be possible to change the opening size of a single rocket slightly by using a drill. Drill the hole under adult supervision and be careful not to ruin the rocket. You cannot decrease the nozzle size after you increase it.

3. Do any changes occur when the rocket is fired at

an angle? If so, why? Support your explanation with facts.

4. Try changing the viscosity of the water by adding a little soap to it. Does this change the way the rocket flies? What would happen if you used something more viscous, like salad oil? Make some general predictions about the relationship between viscosity and rocket performance. Investigate your predictions by experimentation.

5. Using what you have learned from your experiments, find the amount of water which allows the rocket to rise the highest.

6. Design a rocket launch with a given pressure and mass of water that will fly a certain distance when fired at a 45-degree angle.

DO THE FOLLOWING THREE PROJECTS ONLY UNDER QUALIFIED ADULT SUPERVISION AND FOLLOW THE MANUFACTURER'S INSTRUCTIONS. SERIOUS INJURY MAY RESULT OTHERWISE.

7. If you know how fuel-burning rockets work, examine how the amount of fuel and the rate at which it burns affect the rocket's flight. *Note:* Measuring the height to which the rocket rises may be difficult.

8. Using different fuel-burning rocket engines and the results of your water rocket experiments, see if you can predict how the differences in nozzzle size will affect the rocket's performance.

9. Varying the mass of the fuel-burning rocket and using the results of your water rocket experiments, see if you can predict the changes in the rocket performance.

Note: When you present any or all of the above experiments as a science project, include a description of the procedure you used and what you found as a result of your testing. Graphs are useful in presenting the way that pressure, rocket mass, and amount of fuel are related to the height the rocket rises. Pictures or drawings of your test rockets are also appropriate.

TAKEOFF OF A FUEL-POWERED MODEL ROCKET.

AIR FRICTION

Air friction is a force which opposes motion. It affects all motion on Earth; its strength depends on an object's shape and the velocity with which air moves past it. For example, about 90 percent of the energy used to pedal a ten-speed bicycle at 10 m/sec (20 miles per hour) is lost to air friction. When riding at 2 m/sec (4 miles per hour), only about 4 percent of that energy is lost to air friction. Air friction also reduces fuel mileage in cars, rockets, and planes. Engineers work to reduce air friction, and you too can perform experiments to investigate how to reduce air friction.

A CORVETTE BEING TESTED IN A WIND TUNNEL.

In order to do any research with air friction, you need an area of uniformly moving air where you place a model. The best way to do this is to build a simple wind tunnel to find how the air friction varies with the shape of the object and the speed of the wind. A wind tunnel is a long, large-diameter tube in which air moves uniformly. Here, to begin with, are some preliminary investigations.

Materials and Tools

duct tape
cardboard from large cardboard boxes
fan, at least 50 cm (18 inches) in diameter, with two or three speeds if possible
wire screen with 1-cm (½-inch) mesh, and slightly larger than the diameter of the fan
wood dowel, 1 cm x 40 cm (⅜ inch x 18 inches)
modeling clay

spring
6 1-inch nails
board, 15 cm x 30 cm (6 inches x 12 inches)
scale
stopwatch which measures to tenths or hundredths of
seconds

Use the tape to form a tunnel out of the cardboard. The tunnel should be at least four times as long as the diameter of the fan. It must be sturdy enough so it doesn't vibrate when the fan is turned on. Place the wire screen about 30 cm (1 foot) from the fan to help reduce rotation of the air (see Figure 8).

To measure the force exerted on the model, you must build the necessary device. It must hold the object in the center of the tunnel, about 30 cm from the open end. The model holder should cause as little change in the air flow past the model as possible.

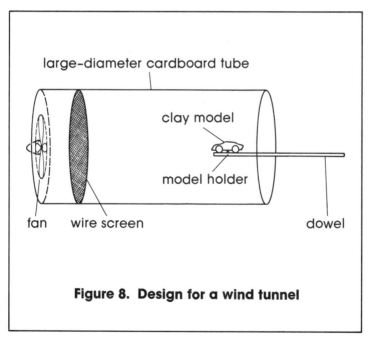

Figure 8. Design for a wind tunnel

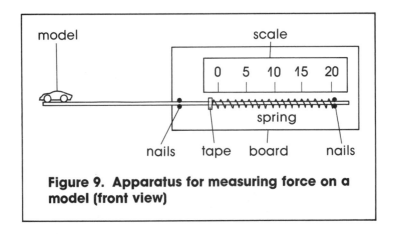

Figure 9. Apparatus for measuring force on a model (front view)

Use the modeling clay to build a model car (or other object, for example, an airplane or airplane wing) about 8 cm (3 inches) long. Place the model at one end of the dowel. Fit the other end of the dowel into the spring, which has been fastened to the board with nails. The dowel is also held in place by two nails and pushes on the spring because of a ring of tape that is a larger diameter than the spring. See Figure 9.

Use the spring scale to calibrate your spring and make a scale relating force and distance for your spring. The scale is made by putting known forces on the spring and marking the position which corresponds to that force. Note: A spring stretches twice the distance when twice the force is exerted on it unless it is stretched too far. The spring is stretched too far if it does not come back to its original shape.

The spring should stretch quite easily in order to find small differences in force. A 4-newton* force should stretch the spring 10 cm. Measure the force by observing how much the spring is stretched, and compare this stretching to how much it stretches with a known force.

*The newton is the metric unit of force. One newton is the amount of force needed to accelerate a 1-kg object 1 meter per second per second.

The dowel which will support your model has some force exerted on it by the air moving past it when no model is present. The force is different for different air speeds and must be subtracted from your measurements to find the frictional force on the model alone.

Measure the air speed for each fan setting by timing how long it takes a small piece of paper to travel the length of the tunnel. Repeat the timing a number of times and use the average value. Divide the length of the tunnel by the time it takes to travel the distance. Avoid adding your "reaction time" into the total time by reacting to start the clock as well as reacting to stop it. In this way, you start the clock late and end it late with each "lateness" of about the same duration. Even though this method for finding velocity is imprecise because the travel time is short, for simple projects it is acceptable.

STREAMLINING IS AN IMPORTANT PART OF A CAR'S
DESIGN. STREAMLINING IS USUALLY ARTISTICALLY
PLEASING, AND IT IMPROVES GAS MILEAGE.

A TECHNIQUE CALLED HOLOGRAPHIC INTERFEROMETRY WAS
USED TO PRODUCE THIS PICTURE OF THE AIRFOIL SECTION OF
AN AIRCRAFT WING IN A WIND TUNNEL. THE DARK, IRREGULAR
LINES REPRESENT AIR DENSITY. SCIENTISTS CAN USE THIS
INFORMATION TO FIND THE AIR SPEED AROUND THE AIRFOIL.

As you begin your investigation of air friction, look at
the difference between smooth, or *laminar*, flow and
rough, or *turbulent*, flow. With laminar flow, air friction is
related to the cross-sectional area (the area that you
see in profile) and the square of the air speed. For turbulent flow, the force is larger. This is why "streamlining" is
important for cars and airplanes, because streamlining
creates laminar flow. Figure 10 shows the difference
between laminar and turbulent flow.

Place a small disk of modeling clay 5 cm (2 inches) in
diameter at the end of the dowel in the "test" position
and find the force at various wind speeds. Then stream-
line the disk by placing two cones of modeling clay on it,
one facing forward and the other backward. Find the difference in the force. Then, improve the cones by round-
ing the edges (see Figure 11).

Modeling clay is useful for making models because it
can be made into new shapes quickly. This allows you to

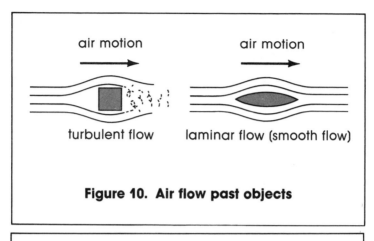

Figure 10. Air flow past objects

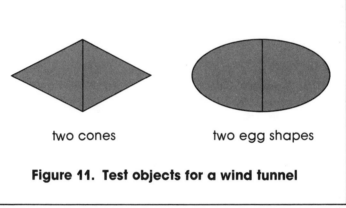

Figure 11. Test objects for a wind tunnel

test your ideas quickly. For more precise data, more precise building materials are needed.

PROJECTS ON AIR FRICTION

1. Build a model of a small airplane which is not streamlined. Then, develop a design for a streamlined plane, change the model as directed by your design, and test it in the wind tunnel. Now see if you can design an *optimally* streamlined plane. If you build balsa-wood model airplanes,

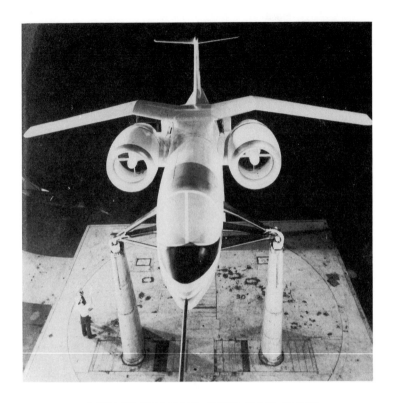

A FULL-SCALE MODEL (WING SPAN 40 FEET,
OR 12 METERS) OF A VERTICAL-TAKEOFF-AND-
LANDING AIRCRAFT DESIGNED BY GRUMMAN.

you might try to modify a kit to your specifications
or build your own working model from scratch—
based, of course, on what you learned from wind
tunnel tests.

2. Make a model of an old square-shaped car and
then compare the forces on it with those of a
modern streamlined car of the same size. Remember, avoid changing more than one variable
at a time. As you make the car more streamlined,
do not change its overall shape. Both cars should

hold the same number of people, baggage, etc.

3. Place a board under a model of a car to simulate a car driving on a road and then see how the roughness of the bottom of the car affects the frictional force on the car.

4. Make a model of an old car mirror with a post and mount it on a board in the wind tunnel. Compare the frictional force with that of a modern stream-lined mirror. Then try to build a more streamlined mirror.

5. After you have learned a bit about how streamlin-ing affects air friction, try designing your own shape for a car that has less air friction than pres-ent models. Remember, the car must still hold people and be the same scale as your other models.

6. Design streamlining for a ten-speed bicycle to reduce air friction as it is pedaled.

7. Design a streamlined shape for a two- or three-wheeled vehicle that can be pedaled by a human.

8. Modify your wind tunnel to measure forces at right angles to the air flow and find how the "lift" of airplane wings is related to the air friction, or "drag." Drag must be overcome by forward force, or "thrust," from the engine. A wing which can lift, or keep the airplane in the air, with the least drag saves energy. Therefore, the higher the lift-to-drag ratio, the better the wing performs.

   Build models and measure the lifting force and the air friction force to find what shapes pro-duce the best lift/drag value. *Hint:* You will find that the angle at which the wing is tilted makes a large difference in the forces. Therefore, make sure you test for changes in angle.

9. Try running similar experiments to the wind tunnel experiments in moving water. Use a swimming pool, the ocean, or a stream. This type of research is done to find the most efficient shapes

for both surface ships and submarines. Frictional forces are larger in water because water is more dense than air, but otherwise the principles are approximately the same as in air. For some people, setting up an experiment in water may be easier than building a wind tunnel.

10. Take a look at some of the designs in the books on paper airplanes listed in the bibliography. Try some of the designs. Use the wind tunnel to help you create better designs for various purposes, for example, acrobatics.

AMUSEMENT PARK SCIENCE AND ENGINEERING

A wide range of projects can be done at an amusement park. These projects probably will not win awards at a science fair, but if your reason to work on a project is to learn, this might be a fun way to do it.

These projects require access to an amusement park because you "borrow" their rides for your experiments. You do need your own measuring devices, but you do not have to build a roller coaster. Some of your analysis will be subjective, but with some thought, you can arrive at valid conclusions.

You might start by trying to define what rides are "scary" and what makes them that way. Some people travel around the United States and rate roller coasters. Their scale is based on subjective data, but certain aspects of the ride are given numbers which are used to arrive at a rating.

THE NORTHROP B-35 FLYING WING. WHAT IS THE PURPOSE OF SUCH A LARGE WING? DO YOU THINK THIS PLANE WOULD BE FAST? TEST THE VALIDITY OF YOUR HUNCHES.

At the amusement park, you might examine the rides which cause weird or scary sensations and figure out why they cause these feelings. Let us say a roller coaster drops very quickly and causes a "weird" sensation. Another ride spins you around and across and you experience another weird sensation as you are pressed into the seat. What about these rides causes these sensations? The analysis requires other rides or other sections of the same ride which give you similar sensations but are not scary.

The rides generally cause you to feel more or less force than you normally feel. Sometimes they take you over bumps, and sometimes they change your rotation rate quickly. The forces are associated with either acceleration in a straight line or centripetal acceleration. (Centripetal acceleration causes motion in circles.) The forces can be measured by taking a small mass supported by a short string attached to a spring scale, onto the ride. If the spring scale measures twice the normal value required to support the mass, then twice the gravitational force is exerted on the object. Sines and cosines can be used to find the horizontal forces from the angle that the string makes to the horizontal (see Figure 12). The equations for these forces are:

$$f_c = mv^2/r$$

for the centripetal force and

$$f = ma$$

for Newton's third law of motion, where f or f_c is the force in newtons, m is the mass in kilograms, v is the velocity in m/sec, r is the radius of the circle of motion in meters, and a is the acceleration in m/sec/sec.

Gravity always pulls down on you, and this force is considered "normal." When you accelerate downward, you feel this force less, so it feels strange. When accelerating upward or going around a circle, you feel more force. Investigate the rides and find when these changes in force occur.

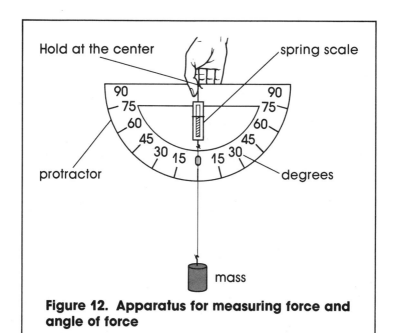

Hold at the center

spring scale

90 90
75 75
60 60
45 45
30 30
15 0 15

protractor

degrees

mass

Figure 12. Apparatus for measuring force and angle of force

Find rides which you think are exciting or scary and then obtain data to compare these rides with less scary rides. Find the velocity, the rate of change in velocity (or acceleration), the turn's radius (if the ride turns), and the angle of bank (if the ride is banked) at the scary points and other less scary points on the ride. Measure velocity by timing how long it takes to go a measured distance. Find the acceleration by measuring the velocity at two points and dividing the change in velocity by the time that it took to change. Distances can be measured by using your pace as a standard unit of measurement. (You might be self-conscious if you walk around an amusement park with a meter stick!)

Measuring heights may be a bit more difficult, but by using a protractor, sines, and cosines, you can find the approximate height. Before you go to the amusement park, make sure that you know the data you need so you can take the required equipment.

PROJECTS AT AMUSEMENT PARKS

1. Roller coasters can be designed so no side-to-side motion occurs, by engineering the proper bank for the velocity. However, such coasters are not "exciting," so designers use different banks to make them exciting. Find places where the banks are not "proper" and see if these spots add to the excitement of the ride. This analysis requires you to work with vectors, velocities, and radii of turns.
2. Investigate how much spinning is good or bad for an average person. Examine the radius of the circle and the rate at which the ride spins. Generally, a number of spinning rides exist at an amusement park so you can compare them.
3. It is possible to measure "fear" by taking the pulse rate and blood pressure of someone during the ride. Many devices are now available to measure the pulse rate with a device strapped onto a wrist. Measuring blood pressure requires the appropriate equipment and permission of the amusement park management. Either one of these methods for "defining" fear may then be used to see which parts of the rides cause people to be scared.
4. Games at amusement parks can be analyzed to see why they make money for the amusement park. Most of them can be won, but the chances are small. You, as an engineer, should be able to analyze why. You also can design your own game.
5. Build a model of an amusement park ride. A roller coaster is an example, but other models can be built. In building a roller coaster, design loops and jumps which "real" coasters cannot have. Ana-

lyzing the motion of your own roller coaster allows you to learn some engineering principles. Start with a single chute, then add to it by putting in jumps and loops and other obstacles for the ball or small car which goes down the coaster. If the car jumps through the air, you learn about projectile motion. If you design a loop, you learn about centripetal force. You may want to take force measurements on the track and measure velocity at various points along the track to see if the laws of physics describe the motion.

6. Examine rides that allow you to experience "free fall" and find how these are rated for being "scary." Also, measure the forces exerted during the fall and after the fall with a spring scale and see if you can explain the results.

GAS MILEAGE

Cars get fewer miles per gallon when driven in traffic than when driven on the open road. You can examine the changes in a car's gas mileage under different driving conditions. Because these experiments do not involve building apparatus, they may not be appropriate for some science fairs. However, a complete analysis of the gas mileage for a car with appropriate graphs and tables can be a good science project.

When working on these experiments, remember that many other factors influence the performance of a car. A poorly tuned engine affects gas mileage as do snow tires, driving in different weather conditions, changing drivers, driving into a headwind, and the load in the car. It is hard to maintain a perfect "control" with this experiment, but with patience you can get some interesting data.

An easy and interesting experiment involves finding the gas mileage for your family car when it is driven under different situations. Keep track of how much gas is used, how far the car goes, and a record of the driving conditions. For example, include the weather conditions, whether it was stop-and-go driving or on the highway, how many people were in the car, and any other information which you think might be important. If you don't drive, have the driver record the conditions under which the car was driven. The experiment must last for a month or so, or until you get data from a number of tanks of gasoline.

For best results, driving conditions should be similar for a given tank of gas. Try to fill the tank before and after a long trip so the gas used for highway driving can be kept separate from the gas used for short trips. Short trips generally involve stop-and-go driving, idling at stoplights, etc. Also, the car must warm up each time it starts, which requires extra gas.

Make sure the tank is completely full each time it is filled. Sometimes, when the tank is almost full, foam causes the pump to shut off before the tank is really full. (A sensor in the pump nozzle shuts off the pump when foam hits it.) Use some standard of "fullness" such as: "When the gas is being pumped slowly, it comes to the top of the tank." Unless you are careful in filling the tank, the actual number of gallons of gas used to go a given distance is not accurate.

PROJECTS ON GAS MILEAGE

1. Test for the effect of driving speed on gas mileage by driving at two reasonably different speeds for a long time. If your car does not have cruise control, it is harder to avoid variability in speed. However, by watching the speedometer at regular intervals, you can get a good idea of how well the average speed was maintained. Differences in gas mileage should be evident with speed differences of 15 km/hr (10 miles per hour) if an entire tank of gas is burned.
2. Find out whether wind speed makes a difference by driving several hundred kilometers (a few hundred miles) into the wind or with the wind on a

windy day. When you drive into the wind, the wind speed is added to the velocity of the car, which increases air friction. The wind speed can be approximated by driving with the wind and finding the speed when no wind passes a hand put out the window. Driving with the wind reduces air friction and should also affect gas mileage.

3. Investigate changes in gas mileage with different loads in the car. Differences in gas mileage are small unless weight changes are large, but four adult passengers instead of one should change the weight enough to see a change in gas mileage on a long trip. Maintain the same average speed during both trips, and make sure that other factors, such as wind speed, do not change between trips.

4. Develop a hypothesis for the change in gas mileage when air friction on the car is changed, and then test your hypothesis. A roof rack reduces the gas mileage, and if something is on the rack it is reduced further. Even opening the windows of a modern car affects air friction because the air does not flow as smoothly over the car. Air friction has to do with how smoothly the air travels over the car and the cross-sectional area of the car. (The cross-sectional area of the car is the "profile" of the car as seen from the front.) A roof rack changes the cross-sectional area and also makes air flow less smoothly.

FLUID FRICTION

The viscosity of a fluid determines how easily a fluid flows. Fluids are either gases or liquids and flow through openings. Molasses is a viscous fluid, water is less viscous, and air is only slightly viscous. (Yes, air—and other gases—is officially a fluid!) Molasses resists flowing through a tube, but it is easy to push air through the same tube. Some substances are used to modify viscosity. For example, soap reduces the viscosity of water, which helps the water penetrate into fabric and clean better. Gelatin increases the viscosity of water.

Viscosity can be studied by using a long tube and measuring the flow through the tube. Flow rate through a tube is related to the pressure difference between the ends of the tube, the length and radius of the tube, and the viscosity. By keeping the other variables constant, the viscosity of one substance can be compared with that of another by observing the difference in their rates of flow. Twice the flow rate means half the viscosity. An equation for fluid flow is given at the end of this section.

Materials and Tools

drill and drill bits
large plastic wastebasket, capacity about 40 liters (10 gallons)
silicone sealant
plastic connectors for joining tubing
vinyl tubing (lawn mower fuel line), 2 m (6 feet) long and about 1 cm (½ inch) in outside diameter
tape
pieces of wood, 1 m (3 feet) long
small bucket, capacity about 4 liters (1 gallon)
small clamp or plug capable of closing the vinyl tubing
meter stick and small scale that measures in millimeters

Drill a small hole in the bottom of the wastebasket. (See Figure 13.) Use the silicone sealant to seal the plastic connector into this hole so it acts as a drain. Attach the vinyl tubing to the connector and tape it to the wood to keep it straight and rigid. Make sure the tape does not change the shape of the tube. Place the wastebasket on a support and make sure the tubing runs horizontally. Place the bucket under the end of the tube. The small clamp allows you to start and stop the flow of fluid through the tube.

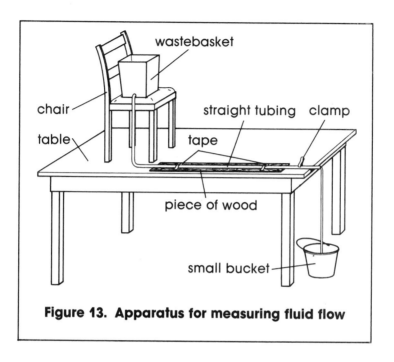

Figure 13. Apparatus for measuring fluid flow

The fluid flows from the wastebasket through the tube and then into the bucket. The pressure difference between the ends of the tubing causes the fluid to flow. This pressure difference is maintained relatively constant by having a large supply of fluid in the wastebasket.

Fluid pressure is related to the fluid's density, the acceleration due to gravity, and the depth. With twice the depth, twice the pressure exists at the bottom of the wastebasket. The pressure at the open end of the tube is zero, so the pressure difference is just the pressure at the bottom of the wastebasket supply tank. With a large supply tank, you can run experiments without adding fluid to the wastebasket supply. With a small supply tank, you must keep the pressure constant by adding small amounts of fluid as it drains through the tube.

First, investigate how the flow rate changes with differences in pressure. Start with the wastebasket half full of water and measure the flow rate by finding the volume of water in the bucket after 1 minute. Then fill the wastebasket to the top to double the pressure and measure the different flow rate.

Next, investigate how the length of tube affects the flow by using a tube half as long as your first piece. Try this for two pressures to see if similar changes occur.

Then change the viscosity of the water by changing the temperature. Water at 0°C (32°F) is about seven times more viscous than water at 100°C (212°F). Investigate this change in viscosity and plot the flow rate for various temperatures and see if the viscosity changes with temperature. Use the millimeter scale to make sure that the diameter of the tubing does not change when the temperature changes. Otherwise, you are changing more than one variable at a time. If the diameter does change, you will have to make a correction using the equation given at the end of this section.

PROJECTS ON FLUID FRICTION

1. Obtain tubing of different radii. Predict the changes in flow rate that should occur. The equation at the end of this section should help you to make a hypothesis about the changes which should occur. Experiment to see if these differences occur with the different-sized tubing. Investigate if the changes in pressure also affect the tubing in the predicted way.
2. Investigate how various quantities of soap change the viscosity of water. Plot the amount of soap against the flow rate on a graph. The results may be quite interesting when you observe how small and large amounts of soap affect the viscosity.

For the following projects, you may not be able to get a wastebasket full of the fluid. Modify your apparatus so that you have a small supply of fluid

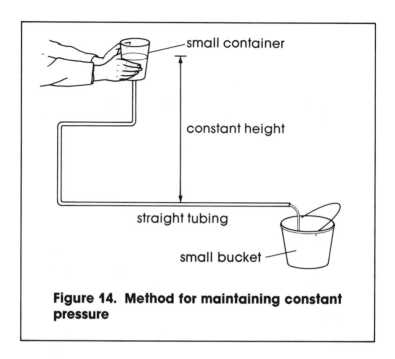

Figure 14. Method for maintaining constant pressure

which can be moved up and down to maintain the same pressure. Connect the supply to the straight tubing with a tube about twice the diameter of the straight tube. As you run your experiment, move the supply to maintain the same difference in height throughout the experiment (see Figure 14).

3. Try other fluids and find their viscosity. You must be careful, however, with these experiments. **UNDER NO CIRCUMSTANCES SHOULD YOU USE FLUIDS WHICH ARE FLAMMABLE, EXPLOSIVE, OR CORROSIVE**. Good fluids are food products such as salad oil, vinegar, and milk.

4. Investigate how motor oil changes viscosity with temperature. Be careful in doing this experiment. Heat the oil only by placing it in hot water. **DO NOT HEAT MOTOR OIL OVER A FLAME. DO NOT**

HEAT IT ABOVE THE BOILING POINT OF WATER. Also be careful to avoid spilling the oil because of the mess that it makes. Try different kinds of oil—10W, 40W, and 10W-40. (W stands for weight. The larger the number, the thicker and heavier the oil.) The 10W-40 oil has the properties of a lightweight (10W) oil when cold. This makes it easy for a cold engine to turn over. When hot, it changes so it has the viscosity of a heavyweight (40W) oil. High-viscosity oil lubricates better than low-viscosity oil. Plot the flow rate versus temperature for these three types of oil and see how they behave.

5. Find the concentration of soap in water that gives the greatest flow rate (lowest viscosity). See if changes in temperature affect the result.

6. Build an apparatus to find the rate at which an object falls through a fluid. This rate is related to the viscosity of the fluid. You may be able to compare viscosity rates in this manner. Your results will be better if you drop a smooth, round object like a small ball.

Note: The equation for the flow rate through a tube is given by an equation. This equation can be used to find the flow rate through your tube:

$$V/t = r^4 \rho g h / 8 \eta l$$

where V/t is the volume flow per unit time in m^3/sec, r is the radius in meters, ρ is the density of the fluid in kg/m^3, g is the acceleration of gravity in m/sec^2, h is the height difference between the top of the supply to the level of the horizontal tube in meters, η is the viscosity in newton $\cdot$ sec/m^2, and l is the length in meters.

ADDITIONAL PROJECTS ON FORCE AND MOTION

The world is full of objects in motion. If you look at something and wonder how or why it works, you might analyze it in an experiment. If you use something that doesn't work the way you would like it to, try to design a better one. Here are a few more ideas for projects in mechanics.

1. Run experiments to find what kinds of snow surfaces provide the least friction. Can you do anything to make the surfaces have less friction? How does the surface change with time? Does its friction increase or decrease? Then, if you can get to some snow, investigate different types of skis and their ability to glide. Try different skis and waxes. From what you learn, see if you can design your own skis.

2. Investigate the way that damp sand stays together in clumps but flows when it is drier or wetter. Sand must be the "right" dampness to stick together, not too wet, not too dry. Initial experiments might be done at a beach, but more precise data require more controlled conditions. Experiment with different kinds of sand, from very fine to very coarse. What factors determine how steep a hill you can make with it? What is required to build a sand castle? Why does it stay together?

3. Investigate how the air pressure in a bicycle tire affects pedaling. Does the amount of pressure affect the comfort of the ride? Remember that tires can take only so much pressure; overinflating them is very dangerous and may quickly become an expensive and very dangerous experiment.

4. Investigate the factors which determine your ability to blow up balloons. Build an apparatus to measure the pressure required to blow up a balloon. Then get data to show why "stretching" the balloon makes a difference. What happens when you try to blow one balloon up inside of another one? Do the differences in pressure agree with what you expect? What is the effect of different sizes and shapes?

5. How does the frictional force vary with different types of materials? Design a tire tread that sticks to the road better than those made by tire companies. Figure out why companies choose the tread shapes they do. What changes are needed if rain or snow is present?

6. How sticky are tapes. How much force is needed to remove a piece of tape? Can you make a tape that is stickier than masking tape? Does the angle at which the tape is pulled affect how it sticks?

7. How does spin affect a pool ball? Does the fabric on the table make a difference? How does spin change with motion across the pool table? Find a better fabric to use for pool tables, one that makes it easier to control the spin.

8. What makes some tops right themselves? Design a new shape for a top that also rights itself.

9. What determines the holding strength of nails? Design a nail that holds better than a standard nail but is no harder to drive into wood.

10. Write a computer program that models the motion of a bicycle down a hill and allows you to vary the angle, the amount of air friction, the amount of pedaling, etc.

4

SOUND

Sound is composed of waves which we perceive with our ears. Because sound is so important to us, scientists have studied sound waves. However, many mysteries still remain to be unraveled, and experiments with sound make interesting projects.

One such mystery is the excellence of the violins built by Antonio Stradivarius (1644–1737), generally acknowledged the greatest violin maker ever. Their sound can't be duplicated by other instruments, and no one quite understands why his violins are so good. Recently, scientists have tried their hand at unlocking the "secret," but they too have failed. Computers and other modern tools seem of little help.

If you work on a project related to waves, you will learn more about how waves behave. Some projects with waves need specialized equipment, so you may have to use equipment from your school science department. However, many projects require very little specialized equipment and only simple tools.

Engineers working with sound waves work in the field of acoustics. These engineers use materials in new ways and try to design structures which transmit or absorb sound waves more efficiently. They often use models to test hypotheses.

STANDING WAVES IN STRINGS AND TUBES

Plucking a string on a guitar creates a standing wave. The standing wave has antinodes, places where the string moves with large motion, and nodes, places where no motion occurs. The large vibrations at the antinodes cause the air to oscillate in large traveling waves or waves with large amplitude. These waves travel to our ears and cause our eardrums to vibrate in standing waves, which send nerve impulses to our brains. This gives us the sensation of sound. A wind instrument like a trombone is basically a tube of air. Standing waves, or large-amplitude waves, are set up in this tube and cause the notes which we hear.

The standing waves that form in the strings of stringed instruments are similar to the standing wave formed in a jump rope. You can think of a jump rope as just a long, very loose guitar string. You can jump over the rope at the antinodes but not at the nodes. The nodes have no motion and occur at each end of the jump rope; the antinode occurs between the nodes (see Figure 15). Vibrations in guitar strings are similar to those in jump ropes but occur at a much higher frequency.

You can design and build your own musical instruments, but first you may want to run some experiments to become familiar with standing waves.

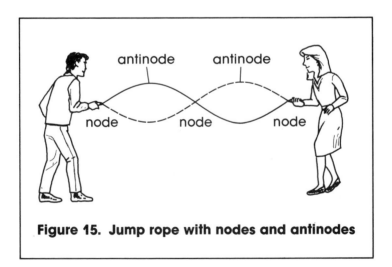

Figure 15. Jump rope with nodes and antinodes

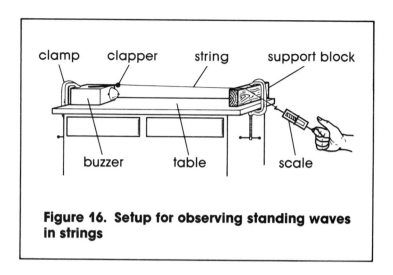

clamp   clapper   string   support block

buzzer   table   scale

Figure 16. Setup for observing standing waves in strings

You can examine waves found in strings by varying the force on a vibrating string. The easiest method uses household string and allows you to easily see the nodes and antinodes.

Materials and Tools

door buzzer with power source to cause vibration at a constant frequency
table
two C-clamps
block of wood, 5 to 8 cm (2 to 3 inches) on a side
household string
small spring scale which can measure 10 newtons (2.2 pounds) of force
meterstick

Clamp the buzzer to one side of the table with a C-clamp. Use the other C-clamp to hold the block of wood on the other side of the table. Tie the string to the vibrating part of the buzzer and run the other end over the block of wood as shown in Figure 16.

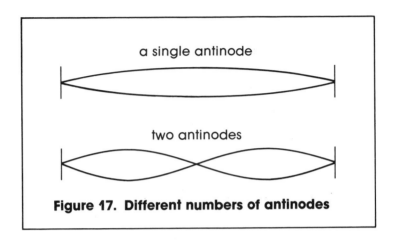

a single antinode

two antinodes

Figure 17. Different numbers of antinodes

Turn on the buzzer, hold the end of the string, and pull gently. Slowly increase the force of your pull and watch the standing waves form, then disappear. Now, attach the spring scale to the string so you can exert a known force on the string. Find the force required to make a standing wave with one antinode, with two antinodes, etc., as shown in Figure 17.

Changing the string's length or thickness also affects how waves travel in strings. Now, change the string's length. What happens to the force required to produce the standing waves you produced in your first experiment with strings?

Next, change the string's thickness by using a double thickness of string or use thicker string. Waves tend to travel more slowly in a string with more mass unless there is a change in force. How much force is now needed to make waves with one antinode? Two antinodes?

Try to change the frequency of the buzzer. This might be done by taping extra mass onto the vibrating part. If you can change the frequency, find how the force required to make one and two antinodes changes when the frequency is changed.

GUITAR STRINGS. WHICH STRING PRODUCES
THE LOWEST SOUNDS? THE HIGHEST? WHY?
CHECK THE VALIDITY OF YOUR GUESSES.

You can also investigate standing waves in a column of
air. All wind instruments produce sounds because of this
kind of standing wave.

Materials and Tools

*sheet of thin clear plastic, about 2 m × 0.3 m (6 feet × 1
    foot)*
cellophane tape
small speaker, 5 to 8 cm (2 to 3 inches) in diameter
cardboard
scissors
small nail

stick, about 1m (3 feet) long and 0.5 cm (¼ inch) in diameter

teaspoon of fine sawdust or lycopodium powder (available in most science departments)

audio oscillator which can produce one frequency at a time (may be available from a school science department)

Roll the clear plastic into a tube so that the speaker fits just inside the tube. Tape the tube along the seam to make it airtight. Place the speaker in one end of the tube, and seal the end with tape. Cut a disk out of cardboard so it fits snugly in the other end of the tube. Use a nail to attach the disk to the end of the stick. (This allows the disk to be moved inside the tube.) Scatter the sawdust or lycopodium powder throughout the tube, and place the tube in a horizontal position. Connect the oscillator to the speaker with the wires.

When standing waves are produced in the tube, air molecules at the antinodes move rapidly while those at the nodes do not move. The moving air molecules at the antinodes push light material until it rests at the nodes. (See Figure 18). Antinodes are in between the nodes.

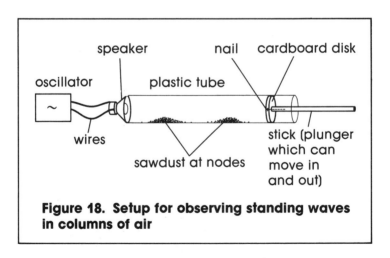

Figure 18. Setup for observing standing waves in columns of air

Set the oscillator at a frequency of 600 cycles per second. Move the disk at the end of the tube in and out until patterns form in the sawdust. Make sure that you get a well-defined pattern. Small changes in length can make quite a difference in the pattern. Now, change the oscillator's frequency. Move the disk in and out until you find a new pattern.

Next, find a frequency and length which give two antinodes. When you have two antinodes, double the frequency and observe the new pattern. Finally, change the frequency to half the value that produces two antinodes. What pattern now forms?

PROJECTS ON
STANDING WAVES

1. Using your string apparatus, graph the relationship between force and the number of antinodes. With very small forces, it may be hard to see the number of antinodes, but the general trend can be found. Next, double the thickness of the string and find out what happens to the graph. Explain your observations.

2. Use a strobe light, available from a science department, to find the frequency of the vibration in the string. The frequency of vibration can be found by adjusting the strobe light speed until you see a single string which is not moving. Find the frequency of the wave with one antinode and a given force. Then, keeping the force on the string the same, change the frequency of the buzzer until two antinodes are found. Find the new frequency of vibration. Repeat this for standing waves with as many antinodes as possible. Explain your results.

3. Using the tube apparatus, find the speed of sound in air. Adjust the frequency and the length so that two antinodes are present in the tube. In this situation, the wave travels the tube's length each cycle. The speed is the length of the tube

times the frequency, or $v = f\lambda$, where v is the speed of sound, f is the frequency in cycles/second, and λ is the wavelength in meters. Multiply the length of the tube by the frequency to find the speed of sound in air. Create some other ways to measure the speed of sound.

4. Find the speed of sound in other gases by using the tube apparatus. **USE SMALL CONTAINERS OF GASES SUCH AS HELIUM OR CARBON DIOXIDE, WHICH ARE NOT POISONOUS OR FLAMMABLE. BE SURE THE ROOM IS WELL VENTILATED.** The gas can be put in through a tube at the speaker end. Generally, you must keep putting the gas into the tube to replace what escapes. These gases are available through chemical supply companies. Use the procedure outlined in project 3 to find the speed of sound.

5. Find the speed of sound in other substances, such as water. What happens to the speed of sound above sea level? Why? Use a vacuum pump to measure the speed of sound in air at less pressure such as at altitudes above sea level.

DESIGNING MUSICAL INSTRUMENTS

Building your own musical instrument can be interesting and rewarding, but you will need patience because instruments take time to build. As you experiment, you can learn a lot about sound waves and about why and how instruments produce the sounds they do. Both wind instruments and stringed instruments can be built. Of course, you can copy some other instrument or even buy a kit to make one, but you will learn more if you build one of your own design.

The tones in a wind instrument are caused by "white noise," the sound of many frequencies. The sound, "sssssssss," is similar to the sound produced in the mouthpiece of a wind instrument. The white noise causes standing waves to occur in the column of air in the instru-

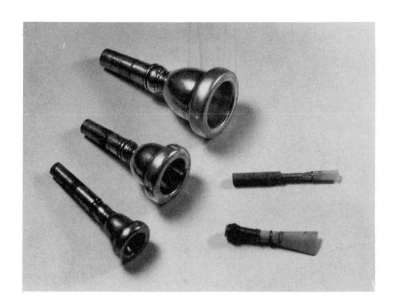

MOUTHPIECES FOR THREE BRASS INSTRUMENTS AND REEDS FOR
TWO WOODWINDS. WHICH MOUTHPIECE GOES WITH THE BRASS
INSTRUMENT CAPABLE OF PRODUCING THE LOWEST NOTES?
WHICH REED GOES WITH THE WOODWIND CAPABLE OF PRO-
DUCING THE LOWEST NOTES? BETWEEN THE LOWEST BRASS IN-
STRUMENT AND LOWEST WOODWIND, WHICH CAN PRODUCE
THE LOWEST NOTE? CHECK YOUR GUESSES BY EXPERIMENTING
OR BY GETTING A DEMONSTRATION FROM A MUSIC TEACHER
OR SOME MUSICIANS IN YOUR SCHOOL BAND OR ORCHESTRA.

ment. Because only specific frequencies form standing waves, only specific frequencies or notes are amplified and heard. The size and shape of a column of air and the pressure of the "wind" determine the frequencies of the permitted standing waves and the amplitude of each frequency. Each instrument produces its own unique mix of frequencies, which we recognize as the tone, enabling us to distinguish between two different instruments playing the same basic note. See Figure 19.

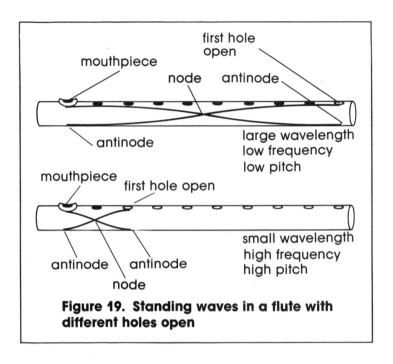

first hole open

mouthpiece

node   antinode

antinode

large wavelength
low frequency
low pitch

mouthpiece

first hole open

antinode   antinode

node

small wavelength
high frequency
high pitch

Figure 19. Standing waves in a flute with different holes open

It is possible to build a simple wind instrument to experiment with how tones are produced. The instrument may not be of concert quality, but it should be able to play a tune or two.

Materials and Tools

1 m (3 feet) of plastic pipe with an inner diameter of 1.5 cm (about ½ inch) (available in hardware stores)
small-toothed saw
30-cm (1-foot) piece of wooden dowel which fits snugly inside the pipe
drill, and drill bits from 3 to 6 mm (⅛ to ¼ inch)
pliers
nontoxic modeling clay
small screwdriver
round file which fits inside the pipe

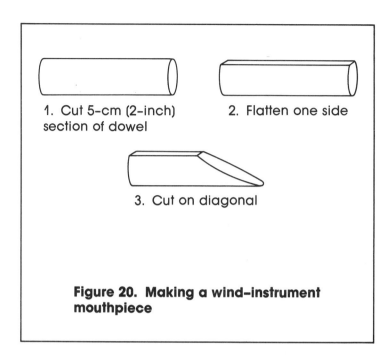

1. Cut 5-cm (2-inch) section of dowel

2. Flatten one side

3. Cut on diagonal

Figure 20. Making a wind-instrument mouthpiece

Cut a 5-cm (2-inch) section of dowel (step 1, Figure 20) and cut off a small, lengthwise section so the dowel is flat on one side (step 2, Figure 20). This cut should be about a tenth of the diameter. Cut the dowel diagonally from its middle to one end as shown in step 3, Figure 20. This is the mouthpiece.

Cut a 30-cm (1-foot) length of pipe with the saw. Then use the saw to cut a small slit in the pipe, 1 cm (about ½ inch) wide and 3.8 cm (1½ inches) from one end, which goes through about one-fourth the pipe's diameter. Push the cut dowel into the pipe so the dowel's cut is centered under the slit. Use a small amount of modeling clay to seal any cracks between the dowel and the pipe at places other than the cutoff section of the dowel. See Figure 21.

The small opening between the dowel and the pipe will enable you to produce white noise. When you blow

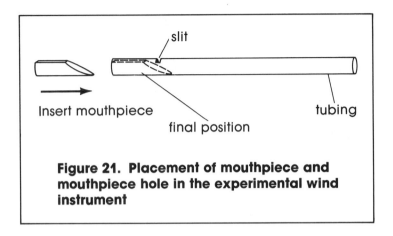

slit

Insert mouthpiece   tubing

final position

Figure 21. Placement of mouthpiece and mouthpiece hole in the experimental wind instrument

into the pipe, air will rush through the small opening and hit the slit. The rushing air produces noise.

Try blowing gently through the pipe. Generally, blowing hard produces just noise, not a clear note. You may get a note at this stage of construction, but you probably will have to bend the pipe slightly to get a good tone. With pliers, bend the pipe right next to the slit on the side away from the dowel. Initially, bend the metal a small amount and see if you get a clearer noise. Increase the bend until you get the clearest note. If you bend it too far and the note sounds worse, it may be possible to unbend the pipe with a screwdriver. The bending helps to make the air flow properly.

Your instrument is similar to a recorder, an instrument which has a flutelike sound. If you are having difficulty getting a sound out of your instrument, you might want to look at a recorder mouthpiece. Seeing one may help you to see what your mouthpiece should be like (see photograph on page 73).

Drill a 0.5-cm (¼-inch) hole halfway along the pipe. Use the file to smooth the inside and outside of the holes. Then place a finger on the hole and release it while blowing. The pipe should make a different note. Make sure

RECORDERS. WHICH ONE CAN PLAY THE HIGHEST NOTES? WHAT RELATIONSHIPS DO THE RANGES OF EACH INSTRUMENT HAVE TO ONE ANOTHER? CHECK YOUR ANSWERS BY CONDUCTING AN EXPERIMENT OR GETTING A DEMONSTRATION.

you blow slowly in order to get a good clear sound. The harder you blow, the worse things get.

Once you have a hole that changes the pitch, investigate hole size to see which size gives the clearest sound. Vary the hole size but make sure the inside of the hole has no rough edges. Use a file if needed. If you make the hole too large, put tape over it and start with a new hole.

After you find the best size hole, place other holes of similar size along the tube until you can play a scale, which is a series of different pitches. Start by covering any holes that you have drilled in the tube and call this note *do.* Then, find a position for a hole for the note *re.* Repeat for the rest of the scale, *mi, fa, so, la, ti, do.* Cover any misplaced hole with tape.

It may take time to get a complete scale. It is easiest to drill holes all along the pipe and then cover them all with individual pieces of tape. Then, starting with the holes at the end farthest from the mouthpiece, remove pieces of tape and see which holes make the proper pitch. Holes that don't make the proper pitch can be covered up again. Repeat the process until you get a scale.

When you have the proper hole placement, use a new piece of pipe, and drill holes exactly where the holes are that created a scale on your first experimental pipe. You have now built your own musical instrument!

PROJECTS WITH MUSICAL INSTRUMENTS

1. Examine the effect of widening the end of the pipe. The wide end of an instrument such as a trumpet or trombone is called a bell. Experiment with the shape of the bell by using either cones made out of paper or larger-diameter pipe. What does a bell do to the pitch of your instrument? How would you "correct" the scale if the bell changed it? Pay particular attention to the "quality" of the sound which the bell produces. Analyze the tone of instruments such as oboes and clarinets. What effect does the bell have? See if you can design a better bell. How would you test it?

2. After you have built one instrument, it is easier to build others. Investigate what happens with larger- or smaller-diameter pipe. Make some generalizations and predictions about what you observe. Test your ideas.

3. Change the mouthpiece shape by using a small cup such as those found on trumpets. See if this kind of mouthpiece improves the sound.

4. Use different material for your pipe and observe the differences in sound quality. Try using plastic tubing from a hardware store, wood, or bamboo. Try some recorders made from plastic and wood. Which sounds better? Why?

5. Design a stringed instrument with one or more strings, and build it. The string, instead of a column of air, provides a standing wave, which is then amplified by the rest of the instrument. In a guitar, the top, which is usually made of wood, vibrates because the string does. This vibration creates the waves you hear as sound. Without the large motion of the guitar's top surface, the strings can hardly be heard. When you buy a guitar, you pay for the "box" (especially the top). You might be interested in buying a kit to build a dulcimer or other instrument. The instrument can be used for your own experiments.

6. Build two stringed instruments and vary the construction methods. For instance, you might change the thickness of the top piece of wood or you might change the material used for it. Listen for differences in sound produced by the different instruments.

WAVE PATTERNS: CHLANDI FIGURES

Chlandi figures (after Ernest Chlandi—1756-1827—a German inventor) are patterns produced by vibrations in flat pieces of material. When such a material is vibrated by a violin bow, for example, sand on the plate moves into characteristic patterns. The patterns depend on the plate's shape, where the plate is held, and where the bow is rubbed.

The patterns occur because standing waves form in the metal. Standing waves form as the waves reflect back and forth in the plate. The waves in the plate can be thought of as having crests and troughs, just like ocean waves. When two troughs or two crests reach the same spot simultaneously, the waves add together to make large waves or an antinode. Other places always have a crest and a trough present at the same time and produce a node.

Sand placed on the plate jumps around at the anti-

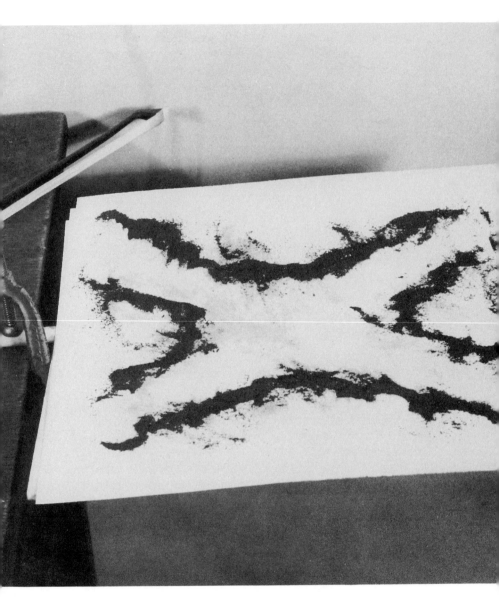

A CHLANDI PATTERN.

nodes. It moves until it gets to a place where there is no motion, a node. Therefore, the nodes "collect" sand and the antinodes "remove" it.

These patterns are fun to make, but they are also useful in learning more about how musical instruments make the sounds they do. Chlandi patterns formed on the back of a good violin make regular figures, while the ones on the back of a poor-quality violin are irregular. By working with Chlandi figures, you can learn how wave patterns form in musical instruments. Using what you learn from the Chlandi figures, you should be able to build a better instrument.

Here are some beginning experiments with Chlandi patterns.

Materials and Tools

hacksaw or metal-cutting saber saw
sheet metal, 30 cm X 30 cm (1 foot X 1 foot) and
    1 to 3 mm (1/32 to 1/8 inch) thick
2 C-clamps
sturdy table
1 cup of fine dry sand
violin bow
drill and drill bits
screws and washers
wood stick, 3 cm X 3 cm (1 inch X 1 inch) and 30 cm (1
    foot) long

A violin bow can be obtained for $25 from a music store or you may be able to borrow one from your school's music department. If you are careful, you won't harm the bow.

Cut a square sheet of metal approximately 15 cm (6 inches) on a side. Clamp the metal with a C-clamp to the corner of a large table. The table should touch the plate at only one point. Shake sand onto the plate and rub the plate's edge with the violin bow. The sand will form patterns. Where are the nodes and antinodes? Record what you see with a drawing or a camera.

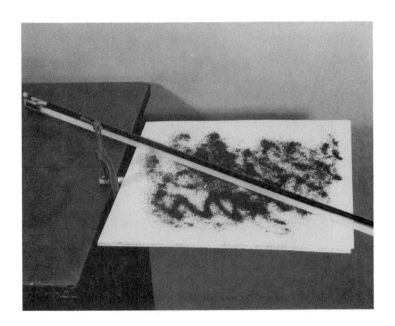

A SETUP FOR EXPERIMENTS WITH CHLANDI PATTERNS.

Next, investigate how different patterns form when the metal is rubbed in different places. Change the clamp's position along the edge of the plate and note the changes. Why did they occur? What changes in the standing waves have occurred?

Finally, drill a hole at the plate's center and use a screw to fasten the plate to the wooden stick. Draw diagrams of the new patterns which form when the plate is rubbed in different places, and see if you can explain why they form.

PROJECTS WITH CHLANDI PATTERNS

1. Change the shape of the plate. What happens? Why do the nodes and antinodes form where they do? Try a circle, triangle, rectangle, etc.

2. Predict what happens if you use two clamps to support the plate instead of one. Run the experiment and explain the actual results.
3. Try to predict what happens to the pattern when you make a particular change in the shape of the metal. Instrument makers make changes in the shapes of their instruments in an attempt to make the standing waves bigger. The larger standing waves cause a louder sound. Test your predictions.
4. A more complex project uses a loudspeaker instead of a bow to generate the standing waves. The speaker is attached to an audio oscillator. The oscillator allows a particular frequency to generate the standing waves instead of the random frequencies produced by the bow. Your science teacher may have an audio oscillator.

   The speaker does not vibrate a metal plate easily, so use a thin sheet of plywood or paneling 3 mm (1/8 inch) or less in thickness. Place the speaker in a small cardboard box, and rest the plywood on the box, as shown in Figure 22. You may need to amplify the output of the oscillator to give a large enough vibration to the wood. A stereo amplifier can be used if you are careful not to damage it. **BEFORE YOU MAKE ANY ELECTRICAL CONNECTIONS, ASK SOMEONE FAMILIAR WITH ELECTRONICS IF YOU ARE GOING TO CAUSE DAMAGE TO EITHER THE AMPLIFIER OR THE OSCILLATOR.**

   Note the patterns on the piece of wood when a particular frequency is played through the speaker. Then change the frequency to twice the original value. Does the pattern change? How do the initial pattern and the pattern with twice the frequency compare? Then make a small notch in the instrument. Is the change what you would expect?
5. Cut wood as in project 4 to form the shape of a violin or other musical instrument. Predict the pat-

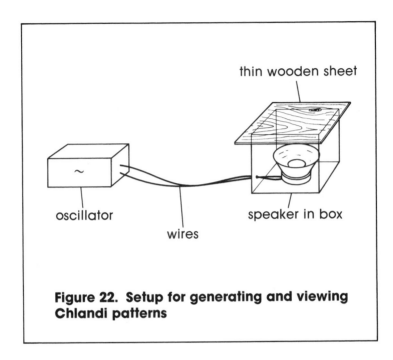

thin wooden sheet

oscillator

wires

speaker in box

Figure 22. Setup for generating and viewing Chlandi patterns

terns which occur at various frequencies before you run the experiment.

6. Start with a well-defined Chlandi pattern formed in one of your pieces of wood. Draw the pattern and then use sandpaper or a planer to make the wood thinner in some sections. Changing the thickness of the wood changes the way waves travel through that section. Will changes in Chlandi patterns occur? If so, what will they be?

7. Try to predict the changes in Chlandi patterns which occur when you make certain changes in the shape or thickness of your wooden plate. If you are building a violin, for instance, it is desirable to get uniform patterns at all frequencies. This makes the instrument sound good at all frequencies. If you do not have those patterns, work to improve them.

8. Although this project may take a long time, you can take your experience with Chlandi figures a step farther. You can build your own musical instrument, such as a guitar. As you work with the wood, make sure that the front and back of the guitar have uniform Chlandi patterns. If the patterns are not uniform, or strange patterns exist, sand the wood so it is more uniform or find a better piece of wood before you have invested a lot of time. Also, talk with an instrument maker, who can give you many more suggestions.

SOUNDPROOFING

Noise is becoming more and more of a problem in our environment. Engineers try to reduce sound by designing materials that absorb sound and therefore make machines and the environment quieter. Many factors affect how sound travels and how much noise reaches your ears.

Flat, hard surfaces reflect sound well and do not reduce noise. Sound-absorbing materials are generally soft or porous. Soft materials absorb sound while porous materials reduce sound by trapping it in small holes. Fabric, for instance, is soft and porous; it is a good absorber when placed on walls. Another efficient material is common acoustic ceiling tile. Sound goes right through the many small holes in the tile and is lost in the area above— never to return. The clothes on your body absorb sound and scatter it: the material has few flat surfaces. The scattered waves are less organized and consequently less obvious. A full auditorium absorbs more sound than an empty one.

Projects in sound reduction can be complex, so you may have to use equipment from your science department. However, some investigations can be done rather simply.

Here is an experiment that looks at the difference in sound absorption in rooms of similar sizes. You will estimate how much sound-absorbing material is in a room and then gather data to see if the amount of material affects the time for a sound to fade away.

Materials and Tools

1 school with a number of classrooms of similar size
2 blocks of wood which can be held comfortably, 1 in each hand
stopwatch

In a building like a school, many rooms have the same dimensions. If a room seems noisier than another, the difference is probably related to the quantity and type of sound-absorbing material present. A room seems noisy if it takes a long time for sounds to die out after they are produced.

Look at a number of rooms and try to list the amount of sound-absorbing material in each room. This list will be subjective, but put things into categories, such as the number and size of wall hangings, and the type of ceiling tile. Most likely, many rooms will have similar amounts of sound-absorbing materials, so you must look for extreme cases. Find two rooms with a lot of sound-absorbing materials, two average rooms, and then two rooms with little sound-absorbing materials. This sample of six rooms is a bit small, but you can still obtain useful data.

Have a friend make a "standard noise" by clapping two blocks of wood together. Use the stopwatch to measure the time for the sound to die away. Have your friend make the noise at a distance from you to prevent the initial loud noise from hurting your ears and making it hard to hear the sound die away.

Timing must be done in such a way that the time for you to react to the sound is the same for each trial. Otherwise, this "reaction time" will cause errors in your data. You can be very accurate if you start and stop the watch according to a set standard. Start the stopwatch as a reaction to the noise and stop it when you hear no noise.

The differences between most used classrooms is probably small, so you may have to purposefully set up

CARNEGIE HALL, IN NEW YORK CITY, IS FAMOUS FOR ITS
ACOUSTICS. IT WAS BUILT LONG BEFORE THE ERA OF HIGH-TECH,
BUT IT PROBABLY HAS BETTER ACOUSTICS THAN ANY HALL DESIGNED
USING MODERN TOOLS AND TECHNIQUES! ONE REASON CARNEGIE HALL
SOUNDS SO GOOD IS ITS SHAPE; ANOTHER IS SOME OF THE MATERIALS
USED IN ITS CONSTRUCTION: PLASTER, WOOD, AND FABRIC.

some conditions. Test a room when all the room decorations have been removed for some reason, say, at vacation. In this way, you are looking at an extreme case. Also try hanging extra curtains or tapestries in a room.

PROJECTS ON
SOUNDPROOFING

1. Using the methods described above, investigate the acoustic properties of your house. This project is easy to do if you are moving into a new house or apartment. In fact, one of the things which bothers people in new homes or apartments is the echoes. With nothing in the rooms, no sound is absorbed and noise reflects easily. With the bare walls, did the designer make the house quiet? How much of a change does adding the furniture make? If any rooms are in shapes other than rectangular boxes, does the sound die away at a different rate in these rooms?

2. If you have access to equipment which can measure the intensity of a sound, repeat the experiments in the classrooms and your house. Your data will be more precise, so you can measure smaller changes in how sound is absorbed by objects. When you add sound-absorbing material to a room, you can also be more precise in measuring the change in sound intensity. Knowing the effect of a particular sound-absorbing material allows you to design quieter rooms.

    The intensity of a sound which reaches a microphone after it is created can be measured with a decibel meter obtained from your science department or perhaps a local government agency interested in limiting noise. Tape recorders also can be used to measure sound intensity, because such machines have meters to measure sound intensity.

    When you use a meter, your standard noise should be a constant-volume noise produced by an amplifier and speaker. Either place the meter well away from the source so the sound must travel a long distance to the meter, or bounce the sound off the walls or ceiling so it gets to the meter indirectly. If you use a tape recorder meter, you must calibrate it in order to get good results. Otherwise, it is hard to know when a noise is twice as loud as another. Talk with someone about how to get reliable data with the equipment you have without damaging it.

3. If you have a meter which measures sound intensity, investigate soundproofing materials with more precision. Design your own materials and test them to see if they absorb sound efficiently. Your materials might be made of paper and cardboard with holes cut into them or they might be cardboard slats similar to those of Venetian blinds. Think about what materials can absorb sound and what shapes can make the sound become disorganized, both of which reduce its intensity.

    Place your standard sound source in one place and put your materials between the source and the measuring device. You might start working with materials similar to those sold as soundproofing materials and then expand your research with your own ideas.

4. Study how auditoriums absorb sound by looking at the amount of sound-absorbing materials in them, their shapes, and the way they are built. Build a model of an auditorium and trace the way waves travel from the stage to other places.

    In auditoriums, places exist which trap sound and prevent echoes from coming back toward the front. Reducing the echoes prevents them from distracting both the audience and performers. One of the hardest places to perform in is a gymnasium with square concrete walls. The sound reflects back and causes problems for everyone present.

After you have studied the shapes of auditoriums and developed ideas as to what makes a good auditorium, build a model of an auditorium and fill it with water. Then make waves in the water where the stage is and examine how the waves move. What changes in the shape can you make to make a quieter room? Note that many auditoriums rise toward the back. This design is used because sound waves tend to rise so sounds rise to the people in the back row. Sounds created by people shuffling their feet rise over the heads of the people onstage, which makes everyone happy.

5. Design a system which would make your gym quieter. The design should be inexpensive, and it also must look good. Would changing the position of the bleachers help? What about hanging tapestries or flags? If possible, try out these ideas after getting the permission of the people in your school.

6. Build an *anechoic* chamber (one that absorbs all sound). Try different materials, for example, egg cartons, cloth, cardboard, or foam. Investigate the properties of such a chamber.

ADDITIONAL PROJECTS ON SOUND

Sound waves are everywhere and you hear them constantly. Things which interest you about how these waves interact are good subjects for projects. Let your curiosity guide you. Following are a number of suggestions for projects. Use them as they are or let them inspire you to think of your own ideas.

1. What factors determine the pitch of your voice and of others? Can you relate measurements of a person's sound-producing system to the pitch of the sound they produce? Find out whether the human voice-making apparatus is similar to a loudspeaker.

AN ANECHOIC CHAMBER USED TO MAKE ELECTRONIC MEASURE-
MENTS. IN THIS CASE, THE MATERIAL ABSORBS MICROWAVES.

2. Analyze the factors that make chalk squeal on the blackboard and then suggest some design changes in blackboards or chalk so that it does not squeal.
3. Find out why shells roar when placed near your ear. Design your own "seashell"—one object of a different shape that does the same thing.
4. Why does a cheerleading horn work? Design a more effective one.
5. Noise from a party tends to increase rapidly as people arrive. Determine what factors cause this, and find a way to prevent it. Design a room that will allow more people to talk without the noise level rising so you have to raise your voice to be heard in conversation.

6. At football games, TV networks use microphones in parabolic reflectors to catch the noises at the line of scrimmage. Can a parabolic reflector send sound in a particular direction as well as pick up sounds from a particular direction? Could a parabolic reflector be used to send plays into a huddle?

7. If you live near a lake, you may have noticed that sound travels long distances over water under some conditions. This effect is related to the temperature of the air above the lake and the way sound waves refract. Find the conditions which allow sound to travel these great distances.

5

LIGHT AND
WATER WAVES

Light waves and waves in water are familiar to us. They have been studied by engineers because of the ways they affect us. Projects in light will help you to understand the way light travels and interacts with objects. As you work on one of these projects, you will learn more about how waves behave.

Engineers working with light, work in the field of optics. These engineers use materials in new ways and try to design structures which transmit or absorb light waves more efficiently. They build apparatus to test hypotheses, and the following experiments and projects allow you to test some of your ideas. The experiments are open-ended, and one question may lead to another. It may be one of these questions which really fascinates you.

A PINHOLE CAMERA

It is possible to take pictures without any lens. A small pinhole in a lighttight box and film are all you require. You can use this equipment to take pictures and also to learn about the behavior of light as it passes through a small opening.

A pinhole camera is a very simple device, but it actually can take good pictures. One of the greatest American photographers, Ansel Adams (1902–1984), took one of his best photographs of Yosemite Valley with a pinhole camera. Although he used no lens, the photograph is equal in quality to that of his other fine photographs.

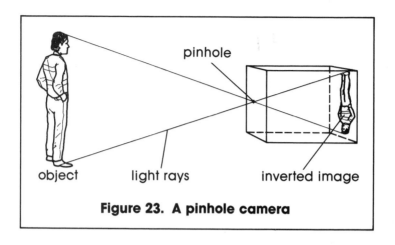

pinhole

object   light rays   inverted image

Figure 23. A pinhole camera

The critical part of taking photographs with such a camera is the pinhole size. If the opening is too large or too small, the picture seems out of focus. Ansel Adams had just the right-size opening! Experiment to find it.

The pinhole size is critical because of the way light waves behave. In a pinhole camera, a ray of light leaving a point on the subject goes through the pinhole (Figure 23). It hits the film at a point which corresponds to the position of the object. With a large hole, a large circle of light appears on the film for each point on the subject. This causes a blurred image because the light circles overlap. With a relatively small hole, however, the circle of light is small enough that the overlapping of circles is not important, although it does give a "soft" focus. Making the hole smaller than this optimum size causes diffraction of light to become important, and the circle of light gets larger.

TOP LEFT: THIS PICTURE WAS TAKEN
USING A 35-MILLIMETER CAMERA.
BOTTOM LEFT: THIS PICTURE WAS TAKEN
WITH A PINHOLE CAMERA.

The phenomena of diffraction occurs when a wave goes through a small opening and some of the light bends. With a very small hole, virtually all of the light bends or is diffracted, and the picture appears out of focus. With a slightly larger hole, a smaller percent of light going through the hole diffracts, making the image clearer.

Let us now build a pinhole camera.

Materials and Tools

shoe box
scissors
masking tape
aluminum foil
pin
film
a darkroom or closet

Use the shoe box as a lighttight box. Use the scissors to cut a hole 1 cm (½ inch) in diameter in one end of the box. Tape aluminum foil over the hole and poke a hole in the foil with the pin. Over the hole place a small piece of tape which can be removed when a picture is being taken. Place the film at the other end of the box (see Figure 24).

The film should be at least 10 cm x 12 cm (4 inches x 5 inches) and can be either regular black-and-white film or Polaroid film. If you use regular film, you will need large-size negative film and must print your pictures from the negatives. This method gives good results. You will need a darkroom and a knowledge of darkroom techniques.

Use Polaroid film if you are not familiar with darkroom techniques. Obtain the kind of Polaroid film designed to be processed *outside* of a camera with special equipment. Try your school's science or industrial arts department for this equipment, or try to borrow or rent it from a camera store.

Once you have chosen a film type, construct a film holder for your box. Then, load the camera in the dark,

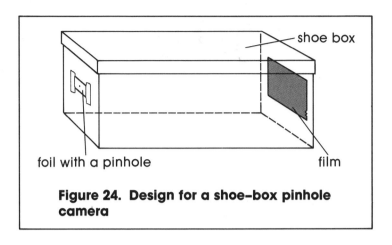

shoe box

foil with a pinhole   film

Figure 24. Design for a shoe–box pinhole camera

close and seal the box, and go to where you want to take your picture. Point your camera at a stationary subject and make sure the camera does not move during the exposure. Remove the tape covering the pinhole, and at the end of the exposure, replace the tape over the hole and process your film.

Start with a hole the size of a normal pin. Initially try exposures of 10 seconds, 1 minute, and 5 minutes of an outdoor scene to give you an idea of how your film and camera behave. Based on this research, vary the exposure time to get the optimum results. Remember, shorter exposure times allow less light in and cause a lighter negative, which results in a darker photograph. In the darkroom, it may be possible to get usable pictures even with improperly exposed negatives.

When you have gotten a good exposure on your film, try changing the pinhole size. Remember, the exposure must be shorter with a larger hole and longer with a smaller hole. Work toward finding the optimum-diameter hole and exposure time for your camera. A hole the size of a standard pin is just the starting point.

PROJECTS WITH
A PINHOLE CAMERA

1. Try taking a picture of yourself. Because of the long exposure times, you can take a picture of a tree and then go and stand next to the tree to be in the picture. When you have exposed the film long enough, return to the camera and replace the tape. You can walk around in the picture and not be seen. You must stay stationary for a long time in order to get a clear picture of yourself.

2. Change the position of the film by moving it closer to the pinhole. What change occurs in the photograph? Shorten the exposure because the light from a larger area is falling on the film. Does the change in photograph agree with what you would expect?

3. What happens if the film is put into the box at an angle or in a half circle? Can you create special effects using this technique? What causes the changes which occur?

4. Make a study of pinhole size versus clarity of the picture. Match pictures equally out of focus because the pinholes are either too large or too small.

LENSES

Lenses are used to focus light in your eye or in a camera. However, no single lens can focus all colors of light at the same place. Different colors of light are bent in slightly different ways because they have different wavelengths. Blue light has a shorter wavelength than red light, and shorter wavelengths are bent more by the lens than the longer wavelengths. This means that blue light is focused in a different place from red light.

Ideally, camera lenses are built so that rays of light coming from the object are all focused at a corresponding point on the film. Because a single lens focuses different colors at slightly different places, camera lenses are designed by using a number of "elements," or separate lenses. This combination of elements allows all colors to be focused at the same place.

Seeing how lenses affect light is an interesting project. Easy projects utilize glass lenses. Other projects involve building your own lenses and seeing how they behave. Lenses can be built out of glass, but it takes a long time to grind the glass. An easier method uses supplies found in chemistry storerooms and hardware stores. Building your own lens allows you to investigate how light behaves in materials of your own choosing.

Here are two beginning experiments. In the first, you will use a glass lens to investigate how it focuses different wavelengths of light.

Materials and Tools

scissors
2 file cards
masking tape
wire screen, 5 cm x 5 cm (2 inches x 2 inches)
small light source (e.g., a 15-watt bulb in a socket)
putty
lens (thicker in the middle than at the edges)
supports for the light source, lens, etc.
meterstick
colored filters

Cut a hole 3 cm x 3 cm (1 inch x 1 inch) in a piece of file card 12 cm x 15 cm (4 inches x 5 inches), and tape the wire screen over the hole. This screen acts as the object. Mount the light source and use putty to mount the file card with the wire screen, lens, and the other file card for the screen in a straight line as shown in Figure 25. You must be able to move all parts easily and measure distances between the parts precisely. You need at least one red and one blue filter (for short- and long-wavelength light), which you can buy at a camera store.

Now, experiment to find the focal length of your lens. During the day, hold your lens near a wall across from a window in a darkened room. Move it away from the wall

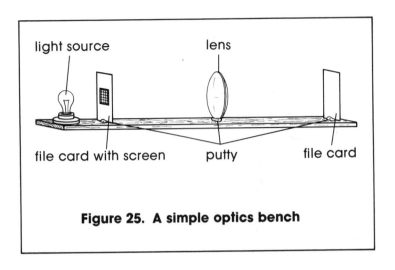

light source

lens

file card with screen

putty

file card

Figure 25. A simple optics bench

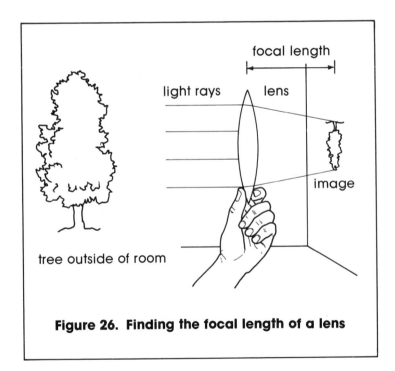

focal length

light rays

lens

image

tree outside of room

Figure 26. Finding the focal length of a lens

until an image of the outside forms on the wall. Measure this distance, which is called the focal length of the lens (see Figure 26).

Again in a darkened room, set up the light source, object, and lens so the distance to the object from the lens is about twice the focal length. Place the screen on the other side of the lens from the object, again about twice the focal length from the lens (see Figure 27). Then, move the screen back and forth until an image of the wire forms on the screen. If you do not get an image at first, make sure that the object, lens, and screen are in a straight line and that the lens is mounted perpendicular to the line connecting the object and the screen.

The positions of objects and the images created by the lens are related to the focal length by a simple equation:

$$1/f = 1/s_o + 1/s_i,$$

where f is the focal length, s_o is the object distance, and s_i is the image distance. Check to see that the object and image distances for your lens are related to the focal length as the equation predicts.

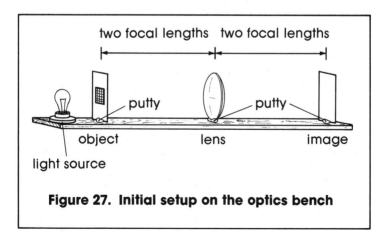

two focal lengths   two focal lengths

putty

putty

object   lens   image

light source

Figure 27. Initial setup on the optics bench

Next, try using the colored filters and see where the new focal point is. The difference in position for the focus is small, about 2 percent of the length, but it is measurable if you make the sharpest image possible.

Once you have built the apparatus used in the first experiment, you are ready to build your own lens.

Materials and Tools

2 watch glasses (shallow curved pieces of glass)
small bucket or mixing bowl
water
grafting wax or silicone sealant

First, build a lens using the two watch glasses. Place them in a bucket of water with their concave sides together. Making sure no bubbles remain in the watch glasses, seal them under water with grafting wax, which retains its sticky properties even when wet. Grafting wax can be found in garden supply stores.

Find the focal length of the lens by using the method discussed in the previous experiment. Now, mount your lens in the same way the lens was mounted in the previous experiment, and find the position of the image. Are the object and image positions for your lens predicted by the formula? What happens when light of different colors goes through your lens?

PROJECTS WITH LENSES

1. Examine how lenses of other materials affect light. Vary the optical properties of your lens by using different sugar solutions to fill the watch glasses. Sugar solutions are safe to work with. Make a few solutions with varying amounts of sugar, including a completely saturated solution (one in which you cannot dissolve any more sugar). This provides you with quite a range of optical properties.

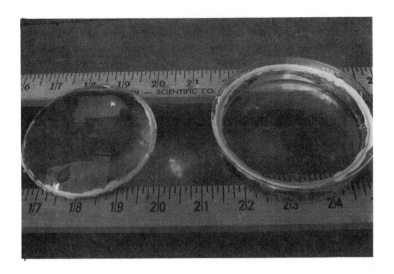

THE CONVEX LENS (LEFT) WAS MADE FROM TWO WATER-FILLED
WATCH GLASSES. THE CONCAVE LENS (RIGHT) WAS MADE FROM
A WATER-FILLED WATCH GLASS AND PETRI DISH.

2. Work with lenses with different sugar solutions and
   look for the different positions of the white, red,
   and blue foci.
3. Use watch glasses of different curvatures to
   examine how lenses of different curvatures affect
   the focal length and foci of red and blue light.
4. If you design camera lenses with all the colors
   focused at the same spot, you will need to work
   with what are called diverging lenses. Diverging
   lenses are thinner in the middle than at the edges
   and do not form an image in the same way as
   converging lenses—the lenses you have been
   working with. To form an image with your apparatus, you need to have two lenses, one converging
   and the other diverging (see Figure 28). Also, the
   optical properties (the strength of the sugar solution) must be different for the two lenses.

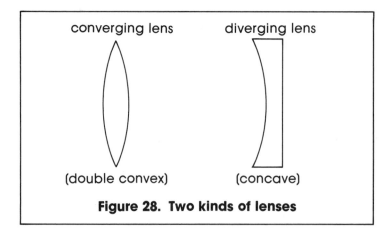

Figure 28. Two kinds of lenses

Build a diverging lens in the same way as the converging lens, except use a watch glass and a small, flat dish called a Petri dish. Place the watch glass so that the center of the lens is thinner than the edges (see Figure 29).

With the diverging lens made with water, use white light to investigate where the image forms when both the converging lens with a sugar solution and the diverging lens are used. (If the diverging lens is too thin in the middle, you may get no image.)

5. Examine where the red and blue foci are for various combinations of diverging and converging lenses. By varying the sugar solutions, work toward having the red and blue foci closer together than their positions with one lens alone. Such a combination makes a better camera lens.

Note: As you work on this project, you will probably want to find out more about lenses. The "lens maker's equation" can be used to design a lens with a particular focal length. Many physics textbooks have this equation and also more informa-

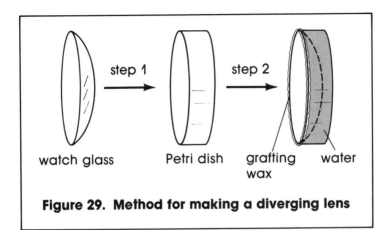

step 1

step 2

watch glass   Petri dish   grafting   water
                               wax

Figure 29. Method for making a diverging lens

tion about the index of refraction and how it relates to lenses. You can do these projects without any idea of why lenses behave as they do, but you will achieve a better understanding of the projects and make quicker progress if you have a better background in optics.

WATER WAVES

Everyone has made waves in a bathtub, so we all have done some minor experiments with water waves. You can also use a bathtub or similar size tank to do some simple but more scientific experiments to learn how waves form, move, and disappear. By working with waves, you can learn how harbors can be made safer and what makes a "fast" swimming pool.

Harbors are designed so that large, dangerous waves are prevented from entering. Jetties—long structures projecting into the water—are often used to break the force of waves, making areas behind the jetty safe from the waves' energy. In swimming pools, swimmers move more slowly if large waves are present. Consequently, fast pools are designed so that waves are prevented from reflecting off the sides. Generally, the wave tops fall down into a gutter and are lost, reducing the reflected wave to almost nothing.

You can build a wave tank and run experiments to design ways to reduce the size of waves. Models placed in the tank are used to test your hypotheses about how to get rid of waves. The tank can also be used to investigate how standing waves develop in a body of water.

Here is a beginning experiment in which you build a wave tank and model harbor to test what is required to protect it from large waves.

Materials and Tools

saw
1 sheet of CDX plywood, ½ inch x 4 feet x 8 feet (1.5 cm x 1.2 m x 2.4 m) (this has waterproof glue)
nails, 1½ inches long
hammer
waterproof wood glue
paint or varnish
caulk
sand of uniform size, pebbles, bricks, and other obstacles
scrap boards

Cut a piece of plywood 4 feet x 3½ feet (1.2 m x 1 m) for the base of your tank. Cut sides 1 foot (30 cm) tall to make a box, the wave tank. Use nails and glue to attach the sides to the bottom. When the glue is dry, paint or varnish the tank. Use the caulk to make the tank watertight. See Figure 30.

Now you are ready to experiment. Move your tank to a place where you can fill it and test it for leaks. Do this in a place where water can be spilled. A driveway is an ideal place to run the experiment. Remember, you must dump the water at the end of your experiments. Plan ahead and prevent the water from damaging anything.

Fill the tank with 5 cm (2 inches) of water and build a harbor of your own design. You might start with a small

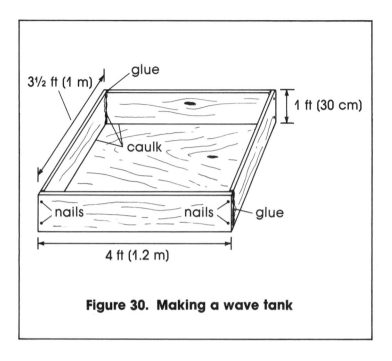

3½ ft (1 m)

glue

1 ft (30 cm)

caulk

nails — nails — glue

4 ft (1.2 m)

Figure 30. Making a wave tank

semicircular bay. Make waves using a small board placed in the water and rapid back-and-forth motion as shown in Figure 31. Remember, you are making a model of a harbor, so the waves must also be to scale. Observe how the waves travel into the harbor and affect the shore. You might put small model boats in the water and see how they move. Make the waves come from a variety of directions because real harbors experience waves from many directions during the year.

Next, with pebbles and sand, build a jetty or two to protect the harbor from storm waves, and test to see if your jetty protected the harbor. Build your jetties so boats can get in and out of the harbor safely without bumping into each other or the jetties. Make waves come from all possible directions. The jetties should protect the harbor from waves coming in any direction.

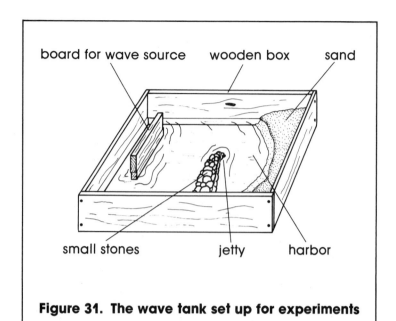

board for wave source   wooden box   sand

small stones   jetty   harbor

Figure 31. The wave tank set up for experiments

PROJECTS WITH
WATER WAVES

1. Is it possible to build jetties which prevent beach erosion? First examine beach erosion by making waves come onto a sand beach from various angles. Large waves are needed to cause erosion. What happens to the sand taken off the beach? Where does it go? Then, construct jetties that prevent such erosion. Can all beaches near the jetty be saved?

2. Make the bottom of your harbor vary in depth. Generally, the main channel is deep and other sections are shallow. See how this affects the way that waves strike the shore. Does the same placement of jetties work for a harbor of varying depth?

3. Change the depth of water in your harbor as occurs with changing tides. Sometimes, during a "storm surge" associated with a hurricane, tides can be many feet higher than normal. Do jetties prevent damage when the water level rises?

4. Build a mechanical wave machine which can produce the same size waves repeatedly. It should be built so the wave size can be changed. With this machine, examine how destruction of the shore is related to wave height.

5. Sometimes it is desirable to have no waves reflected from the edge of a body of water. Fast swimming pools are designed this way because any reflected wave makes it harder to swim. Use your wave tank to test ways to prevent any reflection of waves. Remember, swimming pools must have vertical sides.

6. Remove everything from the wave tank and examine how a sloshing wave occurs in the tank. Lift one end of the tank and watch the wave you create move to the other end. Then lower your end and the wave sloshes back. By moving the tank at the proper time, you can create a large wave. Experiment to see if the time for the sloshing wave to move down and back is related to depth. See if waves of other frequencies can also produce large-amplitude waves.

7. Project 6 can be run in a bathtub, swimming pool, or larger body of water. The difference is that you cannot tip these containers. The water must be displaced to cause the wave. Try making a large-amplitude wave in a bathtub by lifting yourself out of the water at varying frequencies. Which frequencies make large waves? Which don't? How does the depth of water in the bathtub change the frequency? Gather enough data to predict the period of a wave in a swimming pool. The period will depend on the depth and length of the pool.

ADDITIONAL PROJECTS WITH
LIGHT AND WATER WAVES

As you look out on your world, you see light and water waves constantly. Questions you have about how these waves interact are good subjects for projects. Let curiosity guide you. Following are a number of suggestions for projects. You can use them as they are, or let them inspire you to think of your own ideas.

1. What things are required to build a good solar collector, a device which gathers the sun's energy? What color surface works best, and what effect does a transparent cover have on the amount of energy collected? How does the angle of the collector affect the amount of heat gathered? Does the latitude of the collector make a difference?

2. Rainbows, lunar halos, and sunsets are commonly observed phenomena in our atmosphere. Other optical effects include cloud bows, dew bows, sun dogs, solar halos, sun pillars, cloud colors, crepuscular rays, earth shadow, cloud iridescence, the glory, flattening of the sun at sunset, and mirages.

   Atmospheric optical effects are caused by four different processes: light traveling in water drops or ice crystals, diffraction while passing small droplets or particles, scattering by molecules in the air, and refraction as light changes from one medium to another.

   You can use two different methods to examine atmospheric phenomena: (1) collect photographs documenting the phenomena; (2) simulate the effects with apparatus you build. A very complete book about these effects, *Rainbows, Halos, and Glories*, by Robert Greenler, helps you to look for all of these effects and more.

3. Write a computer program which models how two or more lenses behave. Such lens systems are

used in telescopes, microscopes, and eyeglasses. Write the program so you can vary the focal length and separation distances of the lenses.

4. Investigate mirages. A common mirage is the "water" seen on hot pavement. As you approach, the "water" disappears and all you see is the hot pavement. The "water" appears because of refraction of light, but what conditions are required for the refraction to occur?

5. Waves are produced at the front of a boat that are similar to the shock waves that occur as something travels faster than the speed of sound. Investigate how these waves form and travel through water. What conditions are needed for them to form? Does the depth of the water affect the way they form?

6. In a wave tank, build two-dimensional "lenses" which will bend water waves to a focus. These should be shallow areas in the shape of the cross section of waves.

6

THE PHYSICS OLYMPICS

In 1975, Dr. Robert Lillich had the idea of a physics olympics and held the first one at Indiana University of Pennsylvania. Since that time, many such events have been held. At a physics olympics, teams develop individual approaches to solve problems and then test them. The most successful design, scoring the most points, wins.

Physics olympics projects are simpler than those in the rest of this book, but they are educational as well as fun. A classic event in a physics olympics is the egg drop competition. This event involves designing an apparatus from a given set of materials that will prevent an egg from breaking when it is dropped from a specified height. You can work on these designs by yourself, but it is more fun to compete with others. Therefore, you might organize a physics olympics at your school.

When engineers try to solve a problem, they develop a hypothesis and build an apparatus which allows them to test the hypothesis. Then, they experiment to see if their hypothesis was correct. In a competition, many events require you to do this in a limited amount of time—a few minutes or a few days. Arriving at a solution requires you to use your intuition and scientific knowledge. The competition allows you to see the results of your work quickly and compare your ideas with those of others.

RUNNING A PHYSICS OLYMPICS

If you are interested in running a physics olympics, you will need the help of a teacher. The teacher can help you work out the structure with other teachers and the school administration. Your job then will be to organize the people to help run the events. The combination of students and teachers can make the event run smoothly.

A few guidelines are needed for running a physics olympics. You need a list of events, a place for the competition, a method of scoring to determine the winners, judges, and prizes. If you arrange all of these things in advance, the events will run smoothly and will be fun for everyone.

Before you run a physics olympics, you must think about the scale of the event. You may want to involve just your class, all the classes in your school, or all schools in a particular area. With a large event, entrance fees can help defray the costs and provide prizes as well as provide an estimate of the number of participants in advance. Knowing how many people are coming is helpful. Of course, the smaller the event, the easier it is to plan and run it.

The events must be well planned, with unambiguous rules. The rules must tell students the materials that can be used, what determines the winner, and any limitations on construction methods, sizes, etc.

For example, in an egg drop event you need to specify the materials that can be used, the maximum dimensions for the device which holds the egg, the height from which the egg is dropped, the surface used for landing, what constitutes a broken egg, and how the apparatus is dropped. Without carefully defining the rules, there may be ambiguous results and competitors will become unhappy. The materials should be cheap and easily available.

Each event must be located in an appropriate place. For instance, a windy area is inappropriate for apparatus which might fall over in a slight breeze. There must also be sufficient space for both the contestants and onlookers so that people won't be bumping into one another.

Judges are needed to score and run the events. However, they do not need to be scientists because they judge measurable things. The judge's duties include launching paper airplanes, dropping an egg apparatus,

STUDENTS DEMONSTRATING THE PHYSICS
OLYMPICS EGG-DROP EVENT.

AN EGG-DROP APPARATUS.
THE EGG IS COMPLETELY
ENCLOSED IN THE "BASKET."

or measuring the height of structures. The judge's job is relatively easy and can be quite fun, but the judges must be decisive. Their decision should be final.

Prizes might be extra credit, award certificates, or trophies. Exotic prizes are not needed.

TWO SAMPLE EVENTS

1: Egg Drop

Construct an egg carrier that can protect a medium-size egg from breaking when dropped. (Many versions of this are possible.)

1. The container must be made from three pieces of paper and 30 cm of cellophane tape. These materials are provided.

2. The container must be able to pass through a square opening no more than 15 cm on a side. The vertical dimension, measured when the container is falling, may be larger than 15 cm.
3. A strip of paper 20 cm long will be provided and should be attached to the container. The judges hold this paper and release it for each trial.
4. A raw, medium-size egg is provided when you are ready to compete.
5. The judges will drop the eggs from a height of 0.5 m and increase the height in 0.5-m intervals. The surface under the eggs will be cement.
6. Contestants should supply any special instructions for dropping the container to the judges before the eggs are dropped.
7. The egg must free fall the entire distance and survive with no cracks.
8. After each drop, the team may repair the container, but they can add no material other than that material provided.
9. The judges shall determine if any cracks have developed in the egg.
10. The container which prevents an egg from cracking after falling the largest distance is the winner.
11. One hundred points shall be awarded to the team with the largest survival height. The other teams shall be awarded points in a ratio of their survival heights.

Note: Unless the container is required to pass through the 15-square-cm opening, teams can build a parachute and the egg can drop from any height.

2: A Slow Bicycle Race

Ride a bicycle over a course and take the *longest* time.

1. The course is flat, 10 m long, and 0.5 m wide.
2. The course is determined with markers. Hitting a marker disqualifies the contestant.
3. During the ride, no part of the body may touch the ground.
4. The bicycle must start from rest and keep moving forward at all times.
5. Each team is allowed one practice ride and then has two attempts for competition.
6. In the second round, the team order will reverse with the last going first.
7. The bicycle will have one speed and a coaster brake activated by reverse pedaling.
8. The team with the longest time to complete the course receives 100 points. The score of the other teams will be in a ratio to the winning time.

OTHER POSSIBLE EVENTS

Bridges. From a list of construction materials, contestants build a bridge that spans a given distance and can support the largest weight. Another possibility for scoring is to have the supported weight divided by the mass of the bridge. This encourages using less material than the maximum amount. These can be built before the competition or during it.

Airplanes. The contestants build airplanes from specific materials and then fly the planes for distance, accuracy, or a combination of the two.

Boats. With a given set of materials, contestants build boats that will support the greatest weight or can be propelled the longest distance by an energy source such as a rubber band. Aluminum foil and straws are good building materials for these boats.

Wheeled vehicles. Contestants build vehicles out of various materials. The vehicles can be designed for speed, distance, ability to go in a straight line, or ability to haul loads up a hill. The engine could be rubber bands, a heat source like a candle, or wind.

Water wheel. Contestants build water wheels which can do the most work as 1 liter of water falls a distance of 5 cm onto the water wheel.

Paper tower. In this classic event, contestants build a paper tower as tall as possible with a given set of materials, typically a few sheets of paper and a given length of tape.

Balance point. With various masses placed on a meterstick, contestants predict the position of the balance point in a given amount of time. Calculators may or may not be permitted.

Cantilever. With five similar books, contestants design and build a cantilever system that has the largest overhang. The books can be placed in any way to produce the desired effect.

Heating. With a given set of materials, contestants produce the largest temperature difference in a given amount of time using solar energy. This apparatus might be built before the competition.

FOR FURTHER INFORMATION

Contact the American Association of Physics Teachers, 5110 Roanoke Place, College Park, MD 20740, for more information on physics olympics contests; and Science Olympiad, 5955 Little Pine Lane, Rochester, MI 48064, for information on the Science Olympiad.

TOP: A PHYSICS OLYMPICS CAR DESIGNED TO TRAVEL 180 DEGREES AROUND A COURSE THAT HAS AN INSIDE RADIUS OF 1 METER AND AN OUTSIDE RADIUS OF 2 METERS. THE FRONT WHEEL IS TURNED TO GO AROUND THE CORNER. *BOTTOM:* ANOTHER CAR DESIGNED FOR THE SAME COURSE. THIS CAR GOES IN A CIRCLE BECAUSE THE FRONT WHEELS HAVE DIFFERENT DIAMETERS.

7

SCIENCE
FAIRS

Entering your project in a science fair can be a rewarding experience. Some people like to work on a project
just for their own enjoyment, but the work involved in
presenting your results in a competition can help you to
better organize your thoughts and increase overall learning. Also, viewing your project alongside other projects
can be both interesting and educational.

At a science fair, projects are judged on the basis of
originality, presentation, and scientific content. You must
demonstrate that you know the scientific principles pertinent to your project. Your project should be an original
idea. Other people may have done similar research, but
you can approach a problem in a way which is different
from what others have done. The presentation must
allow others to understand what you did, and your data
must offer proof of your conclusions.

When making your final presentation, be sure your
analysis is thorough. Having someone point out a serious
flaw in your reasoning which negates your conclusions
can be embarrassing, and you will be disappointed.

PRESENTING YOUR PROJECT

The actual presentation of your findings is an important
part of your project. The display and written report help
you to organize your thinking and to better understand
what you have done. Both must clearly demonstrate your
methods and results to others.

Make the display eye-catching and include any apparatus you used or at least pictures of the apparatus. Clearly label important parts and explain their functions. Use photographs to document your methods and results. Visual appearance is important because it may be a judge's first impression of your project.

Before you start any writing, review

1. the hypothesis and the design of the project
2. notes on any reading that you did in preparation for running your experiment
3. your data and observations
4. tables and diagrams that you made
5. your conclusions, to make sure they follow from your data.

Writing the report may take as much thought as the project itself. However, it is a necessary part of a science competition, and once you get started, the writing will go quickly. Your report should be similar to any scholarly paper. Include a title page, acknowledgments, table of contents, statement of purpose, and abstract; describe the background for the project, your methods and procedures, and your results; and draw your conclusions. Include a bibliography.

The title page gives the name of your project, your name, your school, your address, and the date. The exact form may vary from competition to competition. The acknowledgments give credit to the people who helped you with information and materials. If you borrowed equipment from anyone, thank them. Also, ask them if they would like a copy of your report. The table of contents lists the sections of the report with their respective page numbers. The statement of purpose is a statement of what you set out to investigate.

The abstract condenses your report into a short paragraph or two. The abstract helps other scientists to quickly get an idea of what you have done. Sometimes the abstract is written last. Two examples are given below:

Changes in Viscosity
with Various Soap Solutions

Steve Smith
Central School
Halfton, N.Y.

The viscosity of soap solutions was investigated and the concentrations of the solutions were related to the viscosity. Viscosity was found by measuring the flow rate through tubes. It was found that viscosity decreased and then increased as a result of increasing the ratio of soap to water. Both pure soap solutions and pure water had a higher viscosity than combinations of water and soap.

The Consistency of
Ski Wax and Friction at
Various Temperatures

John Jones
Mountain School
Mobile, Colo.

A study was made of the physical properties of ski waxes, and these physical properties were then related to the amount of sliding friction on skis. It was found that different properties allowed the minimum friction at different temperatures. Apparatus was built to test the frictional force while the ski was moving at a constant speed and a force equal to that of an average skier was exerted on the ski.

The background section includes information pertinent to your project. Briefly review the reading you have done and the scientific principles that apply to your project.

The section on methods and procedures outlines how you obtained your data. It includes diagrams, photographs, and/or drawings of your apparatus, all clearly labeled. Anyone reading this section should understand how you ran your experiment.

Present your data and conclusions so the reader can understand how you reached your conclusions. Poorly organized data cause the reader to puzzle over how you arrived at your conclusions, and the reader may even miss important data on which you based your conclusions. Also, indicate the precision of your results and whether you think that there is room for doubt. Point out both the strong and weak points of your experiment and make sure you justify your conclusions.

The bibliography is a list of books, articles, and other sources you used for reference. List these sources in alphabetical order by author (with the last name first). Include the following information: last name of author, first name and middle initial of author, title of book or article, where it was published, and year of publication. If it is an article, include the date of the journal and the page number. Often, sample bibliographies are provided by the competition committee. See the bibliography after this chapter for the correct format for books.

BIBLIOGRAPHY

The following books have ideas for all types of projects, suggestions for carrying out your work, or ways to present your project.

Agruso, Susan, Carole Excobar, and Virginia Moore. *The Physics Olympics Handbook.* American Association of Physics Teachers: College Park, Md., 1984.

Ashley, Ray. *Matchstick Modelling.* Topsfield, Mass.: Merrimack Publishers Circle, 1980.

Basic Developing, Printing, and Enlarging in Black and White. Rochester, N.Y.: Eastman Kodak Company, 1977.

Beller, Joel. *So You Want to Do a Science Project!* New York: Arco, 1982.

Benade, Arthur. *Horns, Strings, and Harmony.* Westport, Ct.: Greenwood Press, 1979.

Blaker, Alfred A. *Handbook for Scientific Photography.* Van Nuys, Calif.: W.H. Freeman, 1977.

Boy Scouts of America. *Engineering.* Irving, Tex.: Boy Scouts of America, 1978.

Boy Scouts of America. *Model Design and Building.* Irving, Tex.: Boy Scouts of America, 1964.

Caney, Steven. *Steven Caney's Invention Book.* New York: Workman, 1984.

Ching, Francis D. K. *Building Construction Illustrated.* New York: Van Nostrand Reinhold, 1975.

Cole, Frank, and Charles Wing. *From the Ground Up.* Boston: Little, Brown, 1976.

DeCamp, L. Sprague. *The Ancient Engineer.* New York: Ballantine, 1980.

Derry, T.K., and Trevor I. Williams. *A Short History of Technology.* Oxford, England: Oxford University Press, 1960.

Eastman Kodak Company. *Photography in Your Science Fair Project.* Rochester, N.Y.: Eastman Kodak Co., 1985.

Gardner, Robert. *Ideas for Science Projects.* New York: Franklin Watts, 1986.

Goodwin, Peter. *Physics with Computers.* New York: Arco, 1985.

Greenler, Robert. *Rainbows, Halos and Glories.* New York: Cambridge University Press, 1980.

Halliday, David, and Robert Resnick. *Fundamentals of Physics.* 2nd Ed. New York: John Wiley and Sons, 1981.

Heins, C.P., and D.A. Firmage. *Design of Modern Steel Highway Bridges.* New York: John Wiley and Sons, 1979.

Hunter, Ilene, and Marilyn Judson. *Simple Folk Instruments to Make and Play.* New York: Simon and Schuster, 1977.

Jackso, Albert, and David Day. *The Modelmaker's Handbook.* New York: Knopf, 1981.

Johnson, B.K. *Optics and Optical Instruments.* Mineola, N.Y.: Dover, 1949.

McKay, David A., and Bruce G. Smith. *Space Science Projects for Young Scientists.* New York: Franklin Watts, 1986.

Musciano, Walter A. *Building and Flying Scale Model Aircraft.* New York: Arco, 1973.

Pawlicki, T.B. *How to Build a Flying Saucer and Other Proposals in Speculative Engineering.* Englewood Cliffs, N.J.: Prentice-Hall, 1981.

Reier, Sharon. *The Bridges of New York.* New York: Quadrant Press, 1978.

Roberts, Ronald. *Musical Instruments Made to Be Played.* Leicester, England: The Dryad Press, 1969.

Sawyer, David. *Making Unorthodox Musical Instruments.* Cambridge, England: Cambridge University Press, 1977.

Schulman, Elayne, Ken Craigo, William F. Griffiths, and Denise Megna. *Science Projects with Computers.* New York: Arco, 1985.

Science Olympiad, Inc. *Science Olympiad, Coaches Manual and Rules.* Dover, Del.: Science Olympiad, Inc.

Sears, Francis, Mark Zemansky, and Hugh Young. *University Physics*, 5th Ed. Reading, Mass.: Addison-Wesley, 1979.

Simon, Seymour. *The Paper Airplane Book.* East Rutherford, N.J.: Viking, 1971.

Smith, Norman. *How Fast Do Your Oysters Grow?* New York: Julian Messner, 1982.

Stine, G. Harry. *Handbook of Model Rocketry,* 5th Ed. New York: Arco, 1983.

Strong, C.L. *Scientific American Book of Projects for the Amateur Scientist.* New York: Simon and Schuster, 1960.

Swartz, Clifford E. *Phenomenal Physics.* New York: John Wiley and Sons, 1981.

Van Deman, Barry A., and Ed McDonald. *Nuts and Bolts: A Matter of Fact Guide to Science Fair Projects.* Hammond Heights, Ill.: Science Man Press, 1980.

Walker, Jearl. *The Flying Circus of Physics with Answers.* New York: John Wiley and Sons, 1977.

Walker, Jearl. "The Amateur Scientist," Scientific American, issues 1982–present.

Wenyon, Michael. *Understanding Holography.* New York: Arco, 1985.

Zubrowski, Bernie. *Raceways: Having Fun with Balls and Tracks.* New York: William Morrow, 1985.

INDEX

ABOUT THE
AUTHOR

Peter H. Goodwin teaches physics at Kent School, in Kent, Connecticut. In addition to *Engineering Projects for Young Scientists,* he has published *Physics with Computers* and *Physics Can Be Fun.* Peter is a photographer, glider pilot, and avid outdoors enthusiast—backpacking, gardening, canoeing, and orienteering when he has time. He lives in Kent with his wife, PET (computer), and indoor lettuce patch, in a house he built himself.